Integrated Korean
Beginning 2

ㄴ - money; 길다 — to be long; 단어 - word; 과자; 비밀 -secret; 사전 -con

힘세다 - strong; "안녕히 주무세요" → good night (honorific); 돌아가다 → to return
                                                                    (pass away);

KLEAR Textbooks in Korean Language

Integrated Korean

Beginning 2

Third Edition

Young-mee Cho   Hyo Sang Lee   Carol Schulz   Ho-min Sohn   Sung-Ock Sohn

University of Hawai'i Press
Honolulu

This textbook series has been developed by the Korean Language Education and
Research Center (KLEAR) with the support of the Korea Foundation.

Library of Congress Cataloging-in-Publication Data
The Library of Congress has cataloged the one-volume edition as follows:
Names: Cho, Young-mee Yu, author. | Lee, Hyo Sang, author. | Schulz, Carol
    (Carol H.), author. | Sohn, Ho-min, author. | Sohn, Sung-Ock S., author.
Title: Integrated Korean. Beginning / Young-mee Cho, Hyo Sang Lee, Carol
    Schulz, Ho-min Sohn, Sung-Ock Sohn.
Other titles: KLEAR textbooks in Korean language.
Description: Third edition. | Honolulu : University of Hawai'i Press, [2019]
    | Series: KLEAR textbooks in Korean language
Identifiers: LCCN 2018060911 | ISBN 9780824876197 (volume 1; pbk. ; alk. paper)
Subjects: LCSH: Korean language—Textbooks for foreign speakers—English.
Classification: LCC PL913 .I5812 2019 | DDC 495.782/421—dc23
LC record available at https://lccn.loc.gov/2018060911

ISBN 978-0-8248-8331-7 (volume 2)

Page design by Hyun Jun Lee
Illustrations by Seijin Han

Audio files for this volume may be downloaded in MP3 format at
https://kleartextbook.com.

Printer-ready copy has been provided by KLEAR.

Contents

Preface to the Third Edition

The *Integrated Korean* inaugural volumes, *Beginning 1* and *Beginning 2*, of the Korean Language Education & Research Center (KLEAR) appeared in 2000. They were followed by *Intermediate, Advanced Intermediate* (now *High Intermediate*), *Advanced*, and *High Advanced* volumes. The *IK* series, especially the beginning and intermediate books, have attracted a large number of learners of Korean around the world, especially in the United States and other English-speaking countries. Currently, some one hundred universities and colleges use them for regular classroom instruction. The *IK* series is popular because the authors endeavored to develop each volume in accordance with performance-based principles and methodology: contextualization, learner-centeredness, use of authentic materials, usage-orientedness, balance between acquiring and using skills and, above all, the integration of speaking, listening, reading, writing, and culture. In addition, grammar points are systematically introduced with simple but adequate explanations and abundant examples and exercises.

Over the years, classroom teachers and students, as well as the authors themselves, noticed minor shortcomings in the first- and second-year volumes that called for improvement. Consequently, at the original authors' recommendation, a revision team was formed for the second edition consisting of Mee-Jeong Park (coordinator), Joowon Suh, Mary Shin Kim, Sang-suk Oh, and Hangtae Cho. With a strong commitment to offering the best possible learning opportunities, the team efficiently reorganized and restructured the material based on feedback received from an extensive survey. The second edition of the beginning and intermediate texts and their accompanying workbooks appeared in 2009–2013.

A few years ago a decision was made to improve and refine the beginning volumes to anticipate the needs of today's students and instructors. The following revision team has taken on this task:

Mee-Jeong Park, University of Hawai'i at Mānoa (Coordinator)

Joowon Suh, Columbia University

Mary Shin Kim, University of Hawai'i at Mānoa

Bumyong Choi, Emory University

Several instructors of Korean at various universities in the U.S., primarily University of Hawai'i alumni, have been brought on board to provide editorial support: Sooran Pak (University of Southern California), Jee Hyun Lee (Harvard University), Hye Young Smith (UH Mānoa), Hye Seung Lee (UH Mānoa),

Jason Sung (Kapiʻolani Community College), and UH Mānoa doctoral students HwanHee Kim, Tyler Miyashiro, and Meghan Delaney.

The third edition of *Beginning 1-2* differs from the second in the following respects: First, it features an attractive full-color design with new photos and illustrations; second, most of the conversations have been revised for more natural interactions within each theme-based context; third, some of the grammar points in lessons 2 through 4 have been rearranged to better reflect their level of difficulty; and fourth, the number of total lessons has been slightly reduced by removing lesson 17 and redistributing some of its grammar points to other lessons.

On behalf of KLEAR and the original authors of the beginning volumes of *Integrated Korean*, I wholeheartedly thank the revision team for their tireless effort and dedication.

Ho-min Sohn
KLEAR President
May 2019

Objectives

Lesson 8　서울에서 [In Seoul]

Texts	Grammar
Conversation 1 서울 날씨가 참 좋지요?	1. Seeking agreement: ~지요? 2. Demonstrative expressions: 이/그/저
Conversation 2 말씀 좀 묻겠습니다.	3. Deferential style ~(스)ㅂ니다 / (스)ㅂ니까? 4. N(으)로 'toward N' 5. Irregular predicates in /ㄹ/
Narration　우리 동네	

Culture	Usage
1. Seoul 2. Getting a taxi 3. The subway system in Seoul	A. Conversing and inquiring about someone's 　background B. Asking and giving directions

Lesson 9　생일 [Birthday]

Texts	Grammar
Conversation 1 예쁜 모자를 선물 받았어요.	1. Expressing goal or source: N한테/께 vs. N한테서 2. The noun-modifying form [Adj~(으)ㄴ] + N
Conversation 2 할머니 연세가 어떻게 되세요?	3. Honorific expressions 4. The subject honorific ~(으)시 5. The clausal connective ~지만
Narration　돌 잔치	

Culture	Usage
나이와 생일 (Age and birthday)	A. Talking about important dates B.　Dates, days, and schedules C.　Giving/making/sending and receiving D. Organizing a birthday party

Lesson 10　연구실에서 [At a Professor's Office]

Texts	Grammar
Conversation 1 오늘은 시간이 없는데요.	1. The clausal connective ~(으)ㄴ/는데 2. Expressing desire: ~고 싶다/싶어 하다 3. The sentence ending ~(으)ㄴ/는데요
Conversation 2 늦어서 죄송합니다.	4. The clausal connective ~어서/아서 (cause) 5. The noun-modifying form [Verb~는] + N
Narration　호주 학생 '마크'	

Culture	Usage
서울의 대중 교통 (Public transportation in Seoul) 1. 버스 (Bus) 2. 지하철 (Subway) 3. 택시 (Taxi)	A. Visiting a professor's office: How to start a 　conversation B. Giving one's biographical information C. Expressing reservations D. Making an apology and giving reasons

Lesson 11 기숙사 생활 [Living in a Dormitory]

Texts	Grammar
Conversation 1 차 한 잔 하실래요?	1. The progressive form ~고 있다 2. Intentional ~(으)ㄹ래요
Conversation 2 연극 보러 갈까요?	3. N(이)나 vs. N밖에 4. Asking someone's opinion: ~(으)ㄹ까요?
Narration 캐나다 학생 '민지'	
Culture	**Usage**
한국의 음악 (Music in Korea)	A. Meeting someone by chance B. Extending, accepting, and declining invitations C. Setting up a get-together

Lesson 12 가족 [Family]

Texts	Grammar
Conversation 1 어디서 오셨어요?	1. The clausal connective ~어서/아서 (sequential) 2. Conjectural ~겠~
Conversation 2 가족 사진이 잘 나왔네요.	3. The sentence ending ~네요 4. Irregular predicates with /ㅎ/ 5. The noun-modifying form [Verb~(으)ㄴ] + N (past)
Narration 가족 사진	
Culture	**Usage**
1. 아름다운 한복 (Beautiful *hanbok*) 2. 호칭 (Extending family terms to other social relations)	A. Talking about family B. Ordinal numbers C. Describing clothes D. Describing colors

Lesson 13 전화 [On the Telephone]

Texts	Grammar
Conversation 1 스티브씨 좀 바꿔 주세요.	1. The benefactive expression ~어/아 주다 2. Expressing obligation or necessity: ~어/아야 되다 3. The sentence ending ~(으)ㄹ게요
Conversation 2 박 교수님 연구실이지요?	4. Noun 때문에 5. Intentional ~겠~
Narration 전화 메시지	
Culture	**Usage**
분주한 지하철 (Busy subway)	A. Making telephone calls B. Making an appointment C. Describing illness or pain D. Making a polite request/question

Lesson 14 공항에서 [At the Airport]

Texts	Grammar
Conversation 1 토요일이라서 길이 막히네요.	1. N (이)라서 'because it is N' 2. The negative ~지 못하다
Conversation 2 마중 나왔어요.	3. The adverbial form ~게 4. Negative commands ~지 마세요 5. Irregular predicates in 르
Narration 민지의 편지	
Culture	**Usage**
한국의 종교 (Religions in Korea)	A. Taking a taxi B. Writing letters and postcards

Lesson 15 쇼핑 [Shopping]

Texts	Grammar
Conversation 1 어서 오세요.	1. ~(으)ㄹ 수 있다/없다 'can/cannot' 2. Compound verbs
Conversation 2 이 서점에 자주 오세요?	3. ~(으)면서 'while ~ing' 4. The noun-modifying form [Verb~(으)ㄹ] + N (prospective) 5. The clausal connective ~고 나서
Narration 동대문 시장	
Culture	**Usage**
인사동 (Insa-dong)	A. Asking about prices; buying things B. Expressing frequency

Lesson 16 음식점에서 [At a Restaurant]

Texts	Grammar
Conversation 1 냉면 먹어 봤어요?	1. ~어/아 보다 'try doing' 2. The nominalizer ~기 3. The clausal connective ~기 때문에 (reason)
Conversation 2 육개장이 맵지 않아요?	4. Giving and offering: ~어/아 드리다 5. Negation: ~지 않다
Narration 점심 식사	
Culture	**Usage**
음식 문화 (Food culture)	A. Making suggestions B. Ordering food C. Describing tastes

Main Characters

Mark Smith
*Major in
Korean culture
Australian*

Soobin Kim
*Steve's classmate
Jenny's roommate*

Minji
Canadian

Steve Wilson
*Junior in Music
American*

Lisa
Freshman

Jenny
Biology major

Main Characters

Woojin
Mark's roommate
Korean American

Professor Park
Korean language
professor

Hyunwoo
Soobin's Boyfriend

8과 서울에서

Lesson 8 In Seoul

Conversation 1　　서울 날씨가 참 좋지요?

Conversation　1

스티브:　마크 씨, 서울 날씨가 참 좋지요?^{G8.1}

마크:　　네, 아주 따뜻해요.
　　　　저는 서울의 봄 날씨를 아주 좋아해요.

스티브:　저도 그래요.
　　　　그런데 마크 씨, 이번 일요일에 시간 있어요?

마크:　　네, 괜찮아요. 왜요?

스티브:　저하고 같이 경복궁에 가요.

마크:　　좋아요. 몇 시에 만나요?

스티브:　3시에 광화문 앞에서 만나요.

마크:　　참, 여기서^{G8.2} 광화문까지 어떻게 가요?

스티브:　162번 버스를 타고 서점 앞에서 내리세요.
　　　　광화문은 서점 건너편에 있어요.

NEW WORDS

NOUN

가운데	the middle, the center
건너편	the other side
경복궁	*Gyeongbok* Palace
광화문	*Gwanghwamun*
교회	church
꽃집	flower shop
동네	neighborhood
서울	Seoul
슈퍼	supermarket
약국	pharmacy, drugstore
지도	map
쪽	side, direction
초등학교	elementary school

COUNTER

군데	place, spot
번	number

SUFFIX

~지요?	isn't it? (seeking agreement)

PRONOUN

여기	here
거기	there
저기	over there

VERB

내리다 (내리세요)	to get off
타다 (타고)	to get in/on, ride

ADJECTIVE

깨끗하다	to be clean
따뜻하다 (따뜻해요)	to be warm
조용하다	to be quiet

PRE-NOUN

여러	many, several
이	③ this
그	that
저	that (over there)

NEW EXPRESSIONS

1. 여기서 is a contracted form of 여기에서 (여기 'here' + 에서 'at'). The particle 에서 is often contracted to 서 as in 여기서, 거기서, 저기서, and 어디서.

2. 번 in 162번 버스 is a counter for serial numbers.

3. 광화문 'The *Gwanghwamun*'
Gwanghwamun is the main gate of *Gyeongbok* Palace, which was built in 1399. The municipal government launched the project with an aim to build a signature landmark for Seoul, and as a result, *Gwanghwamun* Plaza opened to the public in August of 2009, after 15 months of construction at a cost of about $37 million.

4. 경복궁 '*Gyeongbok* Palace'
Gyeongbok Palace was the main royal palace of the Joseon dynasty. Built in 1395, it is located in northern Seoul, South Korea. The largest of the Five Grand Palaces built by the Joseon dynasty, *Gyeongbok* Palace served as the home of Kings of the Joseon dynasty, the Kings' households, as well as the government of Joseon.

Exercises

1. With your partner, reconstruct conversation 1 without reading it.

리사: 소피아 씨, 오늘 _____가 참 좋지요?

소피아: 네, 참 좋아요.

리사: 이번 주말에 저하고 같이 _____에 가요.

소피아: 네, 좋아요. _____?

리사: _____에서 3시에 만나요.

소피아: 그런데, _____에 어떻게 가요?

리사: 145번 버스를 _____ 교회 앞에서 _____.
                  그럼 건너편에 _____ 있어요.

소피아: 아, 네. 그럼 3시에 봐요.

2. Ask your classmates for directions to the following places.

A: 여기서 [서점/한국 식당/극장/백화점]까지 어떻게 가요?

B: _____

Grammar

G8.1   Seeking agreement: ~지요?

(1) A: 오늘 날씨 참 **좋지요**?   The weather is very nice today, isn't it?

     B: 네, 정말 좋아요.   Yes, it is really nice.

(2) A: 김 선생님, 내일 시험 **없지요**?   Professor Kim, we don't have an exam tomorrow, do we?

     B: 네, 없어요.   No, we don't.

(3) A: 학교 기숙사가 조용하지요?   The dorm is quiet, isn't it?
     B: 네, 조용하고 깨끗해요.   Yes, it's quiet and clean.

(4) A: 스티브 씨, 보스턴에서 **왔지요**?   Steve, you are from Boston, aren't you?

     B: 네, 보스턴에서 왔어요.   Yes, I am from Boston.

Examples

Notes

1. ~지요? is a request for confirmation or agreement about what the speaker believes to be true. The English equivalent is 'Is that right?' or '. . . isn't it?' In contrast, ~어요/아요? is a regular question that asks for new information without any assumptions by the speaker.

Exercises

1. Fill in the blanks with ~지요? and practice with your partner.

    A: 오늘 월요일 _____ (이다)?
    B: 네, 월요일이에요.
    A: 오늘 심리학 시험이 _____ (있다)?
    B: 네, 있어요. 공부 많이 _____ (하다)?
    A: 아니요, 많이 못 했어요.

2. Translate the following expressions into Korean using ~지요?

    (1) You don't have any questions, do you?
    (2) My umbrella is too small, isn't it?
    (3) You don't exercise every day, do you?
    (4) Professor Kim teaches Biology, doesn't he?

Notes

G8.2   Demonstrative expressions: 이/그/저

[pointing to an object]

(1) 마크: **이** 지도 어느 서점에서 샀어요?
     유미: 학교 서점에서 샀어요.

(2) 마크: (looking at two books in front)
             어느 책이 유미 씨 거예요?
     유미: (pointing to one of them)
             이게 제 책이에요.
     마크: (pointing to one that is on the podium)
             저건 누구 책이에요?
     유미: **저건** 스티브 씨 거예요.

(3) 마크: (pointing to a dictionary on Yumi's desk)
             그 사전 유미 씨 거예요?
     유미: 아니요, **이건** 리사 씨 거예요. 제 거는 집에 있어요.

[pointing to a place]

(4) A: **여기** 꽃집이 어디 있어요?   Where is the flower shop here?
     B: 여러 군데 있어요.   There are several.
          저기 약국 뒤에도 있어요   It's behind the drugstore over there.

(5) A: **여기** 슈퍼가 어디 있어요?   Where is the supermarket here?
     B: **저기** 동네 가운데에 있어요. It's over there at the center of the
          초등학교 옆에 있어요.   town. It's next to the elementary
                                      school.

Notes

1. 이, 그, and 저 indicate the physical or mental proximity of an item relative to the speaker and the listener.

이	'this' (near speaker)
그	'that' (near listener)
저	'that over there' (away from both speaker and listener)

이 책   그 책   저 책

2. 이, 그, and 저 are always followed by a noun.

3. 이것/그것/저것 or 이거/그거/저거: When a thing is mentioned again in the same conversation, there is no need to repeat the noun, which can be replaced with 것/거 'thing'. 것/거 is always preceded by a modifier as in 이것, 그것, and 저것, which correspond to 'this', 'that', and 'that over there', respectively.

것 is often shortened to 거 in casual speech, and further contraction is made when the following particle begins with a vowel:

Full form	Contracted form
이것/그것/저것	이거/그거/저거
이것/그것/저것 + 은 (topic particle)	이건/그건/저건
이것/그것/저것 + 이 (subject particle)	이게/그게/저게
이것/그것/저것 + 을 (object particle)	이걸/그걸/저걸

4. 여기/거기/저기: For places, 여기, 거기, or 저기 is used, where 이, 그, and 저 are built into these expressions, corresponding to 'here', 'there', and 'over there' in English, respectively.

여기, 거기, and 저기 can be used as both pronouns and adverbs of place. The locative particle 에 is often omitted, but other particles should remain.

5. Summary of demonstrative uses:

	이	그	저
thing/object	이 + N	그 + N	저 + N
person	이 사람	그 사람	저 사람
direction	이쪽 'this side'	그쪽 'that side'	저쪽 'that side over there'
place	여기 'here'	거기 'there'	저기 'over there'

Exercise

1. Practice the following dialogues with your partner, using real-life situations.

    (1)   A: [이게 / 그게 / 저게] 뭐예요?

            B: _____ 이에요/예요.

    (2)   A: [이건 / 그건 / 저건] 누구 가방이에요?

            B: _____ 가방이에요.

    (3)   A: [여기 / 거기 / 저기] 뭐가 있어요?

            B: _____있어요.

    (4)   A: [이 / 그 / 저]_____은/는 누구 거예요?

            B: _____ 거예요.

Notes

CULTURE

1. Seoul

Seoul is the capital and largest city in Korea. Situated on both sides of the *Han* River, Seoul, once the seat of the kings of the Joseon dynasty (1392–1910), is now one of the world's largest cities with 10 million people. The Seoul metropolitan area, which includes the port city of Incheon and satellite towns in the neighboring *Gyeonggi*

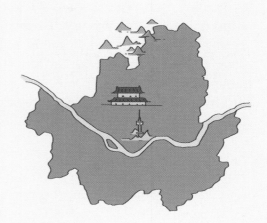

Province is a place where the past and present coexist in a fascinating manner. Centuries-old palaces, gates, shrines, and priceless art objects at museums attest to the illustrious past of the city, while the glistening facades of soaring skyscrapers and the bustling traffic bespeak its vibrant present.

2. Public transportation in Seoul

Like many other big cities worldwide, Seoul has a well-connected public transportation network that is affordable, efficient, safe, and clean. Even if you don't own a car, you can still get around the city and its vicinity without major inconvenience. The main means of ground transportation are bus, subway, and taxi. Recently, public transportation became easier and faster to use with the introduction of 교통카드, an electronic transportation pass. Now you can pay for the bus, subway, and taxi by simply tapping your pass on a receiver.

지하철 (Subway)

The subway is probably the most convenient means of public transportation in Seoul. Seoul's subway network is one of the world's longest with nine central lines in the city area and five additional lines stretching over the boundary of the capital. Line 2, the busiest line, carries more than two million passengers a day, accounting for nearly 40 percent of the population that uses the subway.

버스 (Bus)

There are four different types of buses in the metropolitan area:

- 시내버스: The most common type of bus. They go from one district of the city to another.
- 좌석버스: Express bus with more comfortable seats. They usually run longer routes than 시내버스 and are faster with fewer stops.
- 마을버스: Small-sized local bus. They usually run shorter and more complicated routes within a local area.
- 고속버스: Long-distance express bus. They run inter-city and inter-state routes all around the country. Oftentimes, you have to go to a bus terminal to take them.

택시 (Taxi)

Not like the yellow cabs in New York City or the black cabs in London, the taxis in Seoul come in various colors and types. One exception is 모범택시, a bigger and more luxurious kind of taxi with better service. They are all black with a yellow sign on the top.

Conversation 2   말씀 좀 묻겠습니다.

Conversation 2

마크: 저기요.

말씀 좀 묻겠습니다.^{G8.3}

이 근처에 우체국이 어디 있습니까?

여자: 저기 은행 보이지요?

마크: 네.

여자: 거기서 오른쪽으로^{G8.4} 도세요.^{G8.5}

그리고 쭉 가세요.

그럼 백화점이 보일 거예요.

우체국은 건너편에 있어요.

마크: 네, 감사합니다.

그런데, 덕수궁은 여기서 어떻게 갑니까?

여자: 지하철 1호선을 타고 시청역에서 내리세요.

마크: 네, 고맙습니다.

NEW WORDS

NOUN

근처	nearby, vicinity
덕수궁	*Deoksu* Palace
말씀 *hon.*	speech, words (=말 *plain*)
시청	city hall
역	station
오른쪽	right side
왼쪽	left side
우표	postage stamp
은행	bank
의사	medical doctor
처음	the first time
좀	*Lit.* a little (contraction of 조금)

ADVERB

쭉	straight

COUNTER

호선	subway line

VERB

돌다 (도세요)	to turn
팔다	to sell
묻다 (묻겠습니다)	to ask
보이다	to be seen, visible
뵙다 *hum.*	to see (=보다 *plain*)

ADJECTIVE

감사하다 (감사합니다)	to be thankful
미안하다	to be sorry

PARTICLE

(으)로	② toward, to

SUFFIX

~(스)ㅂ니다	deferential ending for a statement
~습니까/ㅂ니까?	deferential ending for a question

NEW EXPRESSIONS

1. 저기요 (*lit.* 'there') is frequently used as a polite expression to gather someone's attention as in 'Excuse me'.

2. 말씀 좀 묻겠습니다 'May I ask you a question?' (*lit.* I will ask you something) is used as a conversation opener for asking directions as well as for seeking information. 좀, which literally means 'a little', is often used to convey politeness.

3. Directions:

이쪽	this side		오른쪽	right side
그쪽	that side		왼쪽	left side
저쪽	that side (over there)			

4. 덕수궁 is one of the four royal palaces in Seoul, built during the Joseon dynasty (1392–1910).

Exercises

1. Using the campus map below, ask your partner how to get to the following places.

(1)   도서관에서 우체국까지
(2)   운동장 ('schoolyard')에서 기숙사까지
(3)   서점에서 학교 식당까지
(4)   우체국에서 서점까지

Grammar

G8.3   Deferential style ~(스)ㅂ니다 / ~(스)ㅂ니까?

(1)   A: 처음 **뵙겠습니다.**
          제 이름은 스티브 **윌슨입니다.**
      B: 저는 마크 **스미스입니다.**

(2)   A: 언제 한국에 **갑니까?**
      B: 내년 여름에 **갑니다.**

(3)   A: 지난 겨울 방학에 뭐 **했습니까?**
      B: 부모님하고 같이 여행을 **했습니다.**

Notes

1. The deferential style is used mostly in formal settings, for example, news broadcasting, conferences, business meetings, public lectures, formal interviews, and so forth. In general, male speakers tend to use the deferential style more than female speakers, who tend to use the polite ~어요/아요 style even in some formal situations. In broadcasting and conferences, however, both male and female speakers use the deferential style.

2. Even in formal conversational settings, the polite ~어요/아요 style may be used occasionally. This would make the conversation sound less formal.

On the other hand, deferential style may be used in conversations before changing to polite style. In a first-time introduction, as in example (1), the identification of names is usually made in deferential style, particularly among male speakers. Once the communicators have introduced themselves to each other, they may begin to use the polite style. This may be attributed to the idea that before names have been given, the situation is considered formal, because no personal relationship has been established. Likewise, one may use deferential style to speak to a stranger, although many people use polite style.

3. Some fixed expressions are almost always used in deferential style.

처음 뵙겠습니다.	Nice meeting you.
실례합니다.	Excuse me.
죄송합니다/미안합니다.	I'm sorry.
감사합니다/고맙습니다	Thank you.

4. Deferential endings for statements and questions are formed as follows.

	Statement	Question
vowel-final stem	~ㅂ니다	~ㅂ니까?
consonant-final stem	~습니다	~습니까?

5. To express past events, the suffix ~습니다 / 습니까? is attached to the past suffix ~었/았/ㅆ as in the following examples.

일했어요	→	일했습니다 / 일했습니까?
배웠어요	→	배웠습니다 / 배웠습니까?

Note that [N이었습니다] is contracted to [N였습니다] when the noun ends in a vowel, as in 저희 아버지는 의사였습니다 (이 + 었 + 습니다 → 였습니다). Compare 저희 어머니는 선생님이었습니다, where no contraction occurs.

6. The following table compares deferential and polite endings for statements and questions.

Dictionary form	Speech style	Non-past		Past	
		Statement	Question	Statement	Question
먹다	Deferential	먹습니다	먹습니까?	먹었습니다	먹었습니까?
	Polite	먹어요	먹어요?	먹었어요	먹었어요?
가다	Deferential	갑니다	갑니까?	갔습니다	갔습니까?
	Polite	가요	가요?	갔어요	갔어요?
이다	Deferential	입니다	입니까?	이었습니다/였습니다	이었습니까?/였습니까?
	Polite	이에요/예요	이에요?/예요?	이었어요/였어요	이었어요?/였어요?
하다	Deferential	합니다	합니까?	했습니다	했습니까?
	Polite	해요	해요?	했어요	했어요?

Exercises

1. Change the following conversation into deferential style and practice it with your partner.

소피아: 안녕하세요? 제 이름은 소피아 왕이에요.

유미: 안녕하세요? 저는 김유미예요. 소피아 씨는 어디서 왔어요?

소피아: 저는 홍콩에서 왔어요.

유미: 학교 생활이 재미있어요? (생활 'life, living')

소피아: 네, 재미있어요. 유미 씨는 무슨 공부하세요?

유미: 심리학을 공부해요. 소피아 씨는 전공이 뭐예요?

소피아: 저는 아직 없어요. (아직 'yet')

2. Introduce yourself to your classmates in deferential style.

   (1) Nice to meet you.
   (2) My name is _____.
   (3) I am _____ (nationality).
   (4) My major is _____.

G8.4   N(으)로 'toward N'

Examples

   (1) A: 여기서 극장까지 어떻게 가요?
        B: 저기 은행 있지요?
             거기서 오른쪽**으로** 도세요.   From there, turn right.

   (2) A: 여기 이스트 홀이 어디 있어요?
        B: 왼쪽**으로** 쭉 가세요.   Go straight to the left.

   (3) A: 오전에 어디서 만나요?
        B: 시청역 뒤**로** 오세요.

Notes

1.Two uses of (으)로 are (i) means or instrument 'by means of' (G6.1), as in 버스**로** 왔어요 'I came by bus'; and (ii) direction 'toward, to (a place)' as in the examples above.

2. (으)로 is used after a noun ending in a consonant (except /ㄹ/), and 로 after a noun ending in a vowel or the consonant /ㄹ/, as in 우체국으로, 버스로, and 지하철로.

3. 에 is used to indicate a specific destination (G5.1), whereas (으)로 indicates a general direction.

    내일 서울에 갑니다.   I am going to Seoul tomorrow.
    오른쪽으로 가세요.   Go to the right.

    오른쪽에 가세요 is not acceptable because 오른쪽 is a direction, not a specific destination.

Exercise

1. Fill in the blanks with 에 or (으)로.

   (1)   여기서 오른쪽_____ 도세요.
   (2)   A: 유미 씨, 내일 뭐 할 거예요?
         B: 수영장_____ 갈 거예요.
   (3)   A: 생물학 교실이 어디 있어요?
         B: 이스트 홀 4층_____ 있어요.
   (4)   초등학교 앞에서 왼쪽_____ 도세요.

G8.5	Irregular predicates in /ㄹ/

Examples

   (1)   A: 한국 역사를 잘 **압니까?**   Do you know Korean history well?
         B: 네, 좀 알아요.   Yes, I know some.

   (2)   A: 어디 **사세요?**   Where do you live?
         B: 서울에서 살아요.   I live in Seoul.

   (3)   A: 은행이 여기서 **멉니까?**   Is the bank far from here?
         B: 네, 좀 멀어요.   Yes, it is rather far.

Notes

1. When an adjective or verb stem ending in /ㄹ/ is followed by /ㄴ/, /ㅂ/, or /ㅅ/, the final /ㄹ/ is omitted. In case of the honorific ending ~으세요, the vowel 으 is deleted. Then, the stem-final /ㄹ/ is omitted before /ㅅ/: 살 + 으세요 → 살 + 세요 → 사세요.

	~ㅂ니다	~(으)세요	~어요/아요	~었/았어요	~(으)ㄹ 거예요
돌다 'to turn'	돕니다	도세요	돌아요	돌았어요	돌 거예요
살다 'to live'	삽니다	사세요	살아요	살았어요	살 거예요
만들다 'to make'	만듭니다	만드세요	만들어요	만들었어요	만들 거예요

Exercises

1. Change the polite style into the deferential style.

    (1)   저는 교회 근처에 살아요.   → <u>저는 교회 근처에 삽니다.</u>

    (2)   도서관에서 우체국까지 멀어요. → _____

    (3)   학교 서점에서 지도를 팔아요. → _____

    (4)   저는 그 사람을 잘 알아요. → _____

2. Answer the following questions using the deferential style.

    (1) 동생은 어디서 살아요?
    <u>로스앤젤레스에서 삽니다.</u>

    (2) 지금 어디서 사세요?   (3)   김 선생님을 아세요?

    _____   _____

    (4) 집이 학교에서 멀어요?   (5)   어디서 우표를 팔아요?

    _____   _____

4 min.

Narration	우리 동네

안녕하세요? 제 이름은 스티브 윌슨입니다. 저는 미국 보스턴에서 왔습니다. 지금은 서울에서 한국어를 배웁니다. 저는 학교 근처 아파트에서 삽니다. 아파트가 조용하고 깨끗합니다.

이게 우리 동네 지도입니다. 동네 가운데 초등학교가 있습니다. 학교 뒤에는 교회가 있습니다. 교회 옆에는 백화점이 있습니다. 백화점 왼쪽에는 꽃집이 있습니다. 꽃집 옆에는 서점이 있고 서점 옆에는 식당이 있습니다. 극장은 약국 건너편에 있고 우체국은 슈퍼 옆에 있습니다. 그리고 커피숍이 여러 군데 있습니다.

Exercises

1. Read the narration and answer the following questions.

    (1)   스티브는 지금 어디서 삽니까?
    (2)   스티브 아파트는 어디 있습니까?
    (3)   교회는 어디 있습니까?
    (4)   백화점은 어디 있습니까?
    (5)   서점은 어디 있습니까?
    (6)   약국은 어디 있습니까?
    (7)   꽃집 오른쪽에 뭐가 있습니까?

2. Change the polite ending in the parentheses into the deferential ending.

안녕하세요? 제 이름은 스티브 윌슨 입니다 (이에요). 저는 미국

보스턴에서＿＿＿＿＿＿ (왔어요). 지금은 서울에서 한국어를 ＿＿＿＿＿＿

(배워요). 저는 학교 근처 아파트에서＿＿＿＿＿＿ (살아요). 아파트가

조용하고＿＿＿＿＿＿ (깨끗해요). 이게 우리 동네 지도＿＿＿＿＿＿

(예요). 동네 가운데 초등학교가＿＿＿＿＿＿ (있어요). 학교 뒤에는

교회가＿＿＿＿＿＿ (있어요). 교회 옆에는 백화점이 있습니다.

3. Based on the reading, fill in the blanks with the appropriate words provided below.

군데	에서	이게	가운데	꽃집
뒤	왼쪽	약국	근처	

안녕하세요? 제 이름은 스티브 윌슨입니다. 저는 미국 보스턴 ＿＿＿＿ 왔습니다.
지금은 서울에서 한국어를 배웁니다. 저는 학교 ＿＿＿＿ 아파트에서 삽니다.
아파트가 조용하고 깨끗합니다. ＿＿＿＿ 우리 동네 지도입니다. 동네 ＿＿＿＿
초등학교가 있습니다. 학교 ＿＿＿＿에는 교회가 있습니다. 교회 옆에는 백화점이
있습니다. 백화점 ＿＿＿＿에는 꽃집이 있습니다. ＿＿＿＿ 옆에는 서점이 있고
서점 옆에는 식당이 있습니다. 극장은 ＿＿＿＿ 건너편에 있고 우체국은 슈퍼 옆에
있습니다. 그리고 커피숍이 여러 ＿＿＿＿ 있습니다.

USAGE

A   Conversing and inquiring about someone's background

When you want to know about someone's background (for example, the town or country s/he comes from), the question 어디서 오셨어요? 'Where are you from?' is often used (어디서 is a contracted form of 어디에서). The response to this question is [place/location]에서 왔어요, as shown in the following example.

스티브: 저는 미국에서 왔어요.
             마크 씨는 어디서 오셨어요?
마크: 저는 호주 시드니에서 왔어요.
             (호주 'Australia' ; 시드니 'Sydney')

When you specify a town or a city you came from along with the country, the larger unit (country) should precede the smaller (city): 호주 시드니에서 instead of 시드니 호주에서.

고향이 어디예요? 'Where is your hometown?' can be used instead of 어디서 오셨어요?

A: 고향이 어디예요?
B: 서울이에요.

Note that 어디예요? and 어디 있어요? are sometimes interchangeable. However, in the case of 고향 'hometown', 고향이 어디 있어요? is unacceptable. In general, movable objects such as 책 are not used with the copula 이다, but they are used with the existential predicate 있다.

고향이 어디예요?	[O]	고향이 어디 있어요?	[X]
책이 어디 있어요?	[O]	책이 어디예요?	[X]

Exercise 1

Practice the following dialogue with your classmate.

스티브:	안녕하세요? 제 이름은 스티브 윌슨입니다.
마크:	네, 안녕하세요? 저는 마크 스미스입니다.
스티브:	마크 씨는 어디서 오셨어요?
마크:	호주 시드니에서 왔어요. 스티브 씨는 고향이 어디예요?
스티브:	제 고향은 보스턴이에요.
마크:	서울에 언제 오셨어요?
스티브:	8월 24일에 왔어요.

Now exchange the following information.

A: 안녕하세요? 제 이름은 _____

B: 네, 안녕하세요? 저는 _____

_____에서 왔어요.

_____ 씨는 어디서 오셨어요?

A: 저는 _____에서 왔어요.

B: _____ (the place you live now)에 언제 오셨어요?

A: _____년 (year) 에 왔어요.

Practice the conversation again, using deferential style.

Notes

Exercise 2

Let's find out where each student in the chart below came from. Play different roles according to the sample dialogue.

Student	Country	State/town
스티브	미국	보스턴
소피아	중국	홍콩
미치코	일본	도쿄
마크	호주	시드니

스티브: 소피아 씨, 어디서 왔어요?
소피아: 중국에서 왔어요.
스티브: 아, 그래요? 중국 어디서 왔어요?
소피아: 홍콩에서 왔어요.

B   *Asking and giving directions*

When you want to ask for directions on the street in Korea, it is best to start with 실례합니다 'Excuse me', a polite way to seek someone's attention. People will expect this expression to be followed by a question about directions.

(1) A: 저 . . . 실례합니다.
            말씀 좀 묻겠습니다.
     B: 네.
     A: 이 근처에 우체국이 어디 있어요?
     B: 저기 은행 옆에 있어요.

(Note: 저 . . . is used at the beginning of conversation to get the other person's attention, and also for hesitation.)

For more specific directions, you may ask 어떻게 가요? For instance:

(2) A: 여기서 어떻게 가요?   How do I go from here?
     B: 쭉 가세요.   Go straight.
            그럼 오른쪽에 있어요.   Then it is on your right side.
     A: 감사합니다.

(으)로 가세요 'go toward the direction of . . .' is often used to give directions. More expressions asking about directions follow.

오른쪽으로 도세요.	Turn right.
왼쪽으로 도세요.	Turn left.
쭉 가세요.	Go straight.
길을 건너세요.	Cross the street.
사거리에서 오른쪽으로 가세요.	Go right at the intersection.
신호등에서 왼쪽으로 도세요.	Turn left at the traffic light.
극장은 약국 건너편에 있어요.	The theater is across from the drugstore.

Exercise 1

Ask and give directions for each location on the basis of dialogues (1) and (2) above.

(1) 은행　　(2) 우체국　　(3) 극장　　(4) 약국　　(5) 커피숍

You're here.

Lesson 8 In Seoul

CONVERSATION 1   *The weather in Seoul is beautiful, isn't it?*

Steve: Mark, Seoul's weather is quite nice, isn't it?[G8.1]

Mark: Yes, it's really warm. I really like the spring weather in Seoul.

Steve: Me too. By the way Mark, are you free this Sunday?

Mark: Yes, (Sunday's) okay for me. Why?

Steve: (You should) go with me to *Gyeongbok* Palace!

Mark: Great! What time do we meet?

Steve: Let's meet at 3 o'clock in front of *Gwanghwamun*.

Mark: By the way, how do I get to *Gwanghwamun* from here?[G8.2]

Steve: Take Bus 162 and get off in front of the bookstore.
             Gwanghwamun is across from the bookstore.

CONVERSATION 2   *May I ask you something?*

Mark: Excuse me. I'd like to ask you something.[G8.3]
             Is there a post office near here?

Woman: Do you see the bank over there?

Mark: Yes.

Woman: From there, turn to the right[G8.5] and go straight, then you'll
             see a department store. The post office is across from that.

Mark: I see, thank you. By the way, how do I get to *Deoksu* Palace
             from here?

Woman: Take subway Line #1 and get off at City Hall Station.

Mark: I see, thank you.

NARRATION   *Our Neighborhood*

Hello. My name is Steve Wilson. I am from Boston, USA. Currently I am learning
Korean in Seoul. I live in an apartment near school. The apartment is quiet and
clean. This is a map of my neighborhood. In the center of the neighborhood,
there is an elementary school. Behind the school, there is a church. In front of
the church, there is a department store. To the left of the department store, there
is a flower shop. Next to the flower shop, there is a bookstore and next to the
bookstore, there is a restaurant. The theater is across from the pharmacy and the
post office is next to the supermarket. There are also several coffee shops.

9과 생일

Lesson 9 Birthday

Conversation 1 예쁜 모자를 선물 받았어요.

Conversation 1

스티브:	리사 씨, 지난 주말에 뭐 했어요?
리사:	토요일이 제 생일이었어요.
	그래서 생일 파티 했어요.
스티브:	아, 그랬어요? 축하해요.
리사:	고마워요.
스티브:	생일 선물 많이 받았어요?
리사:	네, 친구들한테서[G9.1] 많이 받았어요.
스티브:	무슨 선물 받았어요?
리사:	예쁜[G9.2] 모자하고 책을 받았어요.
	스티브 씨 생일은 언제예요?
스티브:	제 생일은 6월 27일이에요.

NEW WORDS

NOUN

건물	building
돈	money
돌	the first birthday
며칠	what date; a few days
모자	cap, hat
번호	number
올해	this year
이메일	email
잔치	feast, party
카드	card
편지	letter (written message)

SUFFIX

~(으)ㄴ	noun-modifying form

VERB

보내다	② to send
축하하다	to congratulate

ADJECTIVE

길다	to be long
짧다	to be short

PARTICLE

께 *hon.*	to (a person)
와/과	and (joins nouns) 와 after vowel; 과 after consonant
한테	to (a person or an animal; colloquial form)
한테서	from (a person or an animal; colloquial form)

NEW EXPRESSIONS

1. In Korean, dates are expressed in Sino-Korean numbers (e.g., 일, 이, 삼, 사, 오 . . .) in the order of year-month-day.

오늘은 며칠이에요?	What day of the month is it today?
오늘은 2020년 12월 29일이에요.	Today is December 29, 2020.

2. Months of the year:

1월	January	7월	July
2월	February	8월	August
3월	March	9월	September
4월	April	10월(시월)	October
5월	May	11월	November
6월 (유월)	June	12월	December

3. Days of the month:

1일	the first	12일	the twelfth
2일	the second	20일	the twentieth
3일	the third	31일	the thirty-first

Exercises

1. Practice reading the following dates.

  (1) January 1st   (2) April 5th

  (3) June 6th   (4) August 17th

  (5) October 3rd   (6) December 21st

2. Fill in the blanks with your own information.

  (1) 제 생일은 ___사___ 월 _이십이_ 일이에요.

  (2) 지난 크리스마스에 _누구_ 한테서 _선물_ 을/를 받았어요?

  (3) A: 오늘 며칠이에요?

     B: ___오___ 월 ___십___ 일이에요.

  (4) 친구한테 _____을/를 선물할 거예요.

✏ **Notes**

....

....

....

....

....

....

Grammar

G9.1   Expressing goal or source : N한테/께 vs. N한테서

[Person] 한테/께 'to (a person)'

(1) 유미: 리사 씨, 언니**한테** 이메일 자주 보내세요?

   리사: 아니요, 자주 못 보내요.

              유미 씨는 부모님**께** 편지 자주 하세요?

   유미: 네, 자주 해요.

(2) 어제는 리사 생일이었어요.

   그래서 리사**한테** 꽃과 카드를 주었어요.

[Person] 한테서/께 'from (a person)'

(3) 소피아: 리사 씨, 올해 생일 선물 많이 받았어요?

   리사: 꽃하고 책을 받았어요.

   소피아: 누구**한테서** 책을 받았어요?

   리사: 마이클**한테서** 받았어요.

(4) 스티브: 마이클 씨, 선생님**께** 전화 왔어요.

   마이클: 네, 고마워요.

[Place]에 'to (a place)'

(5) 제니: 마이클 씨, 서울**에** 며칠에 가요?

   마이클: 10월 13일에 가요.

(6) 스티브: 소피아 씨, 홍콩**에** 전화 자주 하세요?

   소피아: 네, 자주 해요.

[Place]에서 'from (a place)'

(7) 제니: 서울**에서** 편지가 왔어요.

(8) 스티브: 마이클 씨, 집**에서** 전화 왔어요.

   마이클: 누구예요?

   스티브: 마이클 씨 동생이에요.

Notes

1. The particle 한테 is used with 'giving or sending' verbs while 한테서 is used with 'receiving' verbs.

'giving or sending' type	'receiving' type
N한테 선물(을) 하다/주다	N한테서 선물(을) 받다
N한테 전화(를) 하다	N한테서 전화(를) 받다/ 전화(가) 오다
N한테 편지(를) 보내다/하다	N한테서 편지(를) 받다/ 편지(가) 오다
N한테 얘기(를) 하다	N한테서 얘기(를) 듣다

2. When the recipient is a respected senior (e.g., 부모님 and 선생님), the honorific particle 께 should be used instead of 한테, as in (1) above. The honorific form of 한테서 is also 께 as in (4).

3. The particle 도 can be added after 한테 or 한테서 to indicate 'also, too'.

> 어제 마이클한테 전화 했어요. 그리고 리사한테도 전화 했어요.
> 마이클한테서 이메일이 왔어요. 그리고 유미한테서도 왔어요.

4. While 한테 and 한테서 are used with persons, 에 and 에서 are used with places. The particles 에 (G5.1) and 에서 express 'to (a place)' and 'from (a place)' respectively as in (5)–(8).

Exercises

1. Describe the pictures as shown in (1).

(1)

메리/제임스   메리가 제임스한테 전화 번호를 주었어요.

(2)

유미/리사   유미는 리사한데 책을 줘요 주었어요

(3)

스티브/유미 _____

(4)

리사/김 선생님 _____

2. Fill in the blanks with the proper particles, provided in the box below.

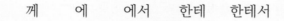

께   에   에서   한테   한테서

(1) 리사가 마이클 __한테__ 전화를 했어요.

(2) 유미는 생일에 스티브 __한테서__ 카드를 받았어요.

(3) 소피아는 로스앤젤레스 __에__ 전화했어요.

(4) 민지는 조카('nephew') 돌 잔치 __에__ 꽃을 보냈어요.

(5) 어제 오빠 __한데서__ 전화가 왔어요.

(6) 부모님 __께__ 편지 자주 쓰세요?

(7) 라디오 ('radio') __에서__ 음악을 들었어요.

(8) 스티브가 크리스마스에 형 __한데서__ 돈을 받았어요.

G9.2   The noun-modifying form [Adj~(으)ㄴ] + N

(1)   우체국은 **큰** 건물 안에 있어요.

(2)   리사는 백화점에서 **좋은** 옷을 샀어요.

(3)   스티브는 시청에서 **가까운** 아파트에 살아요.

(4)   교회 옆에 작고 **예쁜** 꽃집이 있습니다.

Notes

1. ~(으)ㄴ occurs with adjectives and is used to modify nouns, as in 큰 집 'big house'.

Examples of adjective stems that end in vowels:

Adjective stem + ㄴ			
Dictionary form		Noun-modifying form	
크다	to be big	큰	big
싸다	to be inexpensive	싼	inexpensive
예쁘다	to be pretty	예쁜	pretty

Examples of adjective stems that end in consonants:

Adjective stem + 은			
Dictionary form		Noun-modifying form	
좋다	to be good	좋은	good
많다	to be many	많은	plentiful
작다	to be small	작은	small

2. Noun-modifying forms of the irregular predicates in /ㅂ/

If /ㅂ/ is at the end of the adjective stem, it is changed to 우 before a vowel (G6.2).

가깝 + 은 → 가까우 + 은 → 가까우 + ㄴ → 가까운

	Dictionary form	Noun-modifying form
가깝다	to be close, near	가까운 집
춥다	to be cold	추운 날씨
어렵다	to be difficult	어려운 시험
쉽다	to be easy	쉬운 숙제

Examples of regular adjectives in /ㅂ/:

	Dictionary form	Noun-modifying form
좁다	to be narrow	좁은 방
짧다	to be short	짧은 머리 ('hair')

3. Noun-modifying forms of the irregular predicates in /ㄹ/:

When an adjective stem ending in /ㄹ/ is followed by /ㄴ/, /ㅂ/, or /ㅅ/, the final /ㄹ/ is omitted (G8.5). In the following example, the syllable 은 is shortened to ㄴ, and then, the adjective stem-final /ㄹ/ is deleted because of the following /ㄴ/.

멀 + 은 → 멀 + ㄴ → 머 + ㄴ → 먼

	Dictionary form	Noun-modifying form
멀다	to be far	먼 거리 ('distance')
길다	to be long	긴 머리

4. Adjectives 있다/ 없다 take ~는 instead of ~(으)ㄴ.

	Dictionary form	Noun-modifying form
재미있다	to be interesting, fun	재미있는 interesting
맛없다	to not be tasty	맛없는 bad-tasting

5. When you use more than one adjective, the adjectives are connected with ~고 'and', and only the last adjective takes the noun-modifying form, as in 비싸고 좋은 옷 'expensive and nice clothes', 싸고 맛있는 음식 'cheap and tasty food', and 깨끗하고 넓은 집 'clean and spacious house'.

Exercise

1. Fill in the blanks with appropriate noun-modifying forms.

(1) _예쁜_____ 나라

(2) _어려운_____ 대학교

(3) _재미있는_____ 영화

(4) _조요한_____ 동네

2. Translate the following sentences into Korean.

(1) Lisa is a *good* **student**.
리사는 좋은 학생이에요.

(2) I like *large* **bags**.

_____

(3) I bought this present at a *nearby* **department store**.

_____

(4) I bought a *small* and *pretty* **watch**.

_____

(5) I live in a *quiet* and *clean* **apartment**.

_____

Notes

....

....

....

....

....

....

CULTURE

나이와 생일 (Age and birthday)

Many people get confused by the way Koreans calculate age. It is easy, however, if you keep two things in mind. First, you are one year old the moment you are born. Second, you become a year older, not on your birthday, but on January first. This means that a baby born on December 31 will be two years old the very next day after he/she is born.

There are two distinctive birthdays that Koreans celebrate in special ways: 돌 and 환갑. 돌 is the first birthday after one's birth while 환갑 is one's sixtieth birthday. 환갑 is celebrated because it is the first occasion during which the specific combination of Chinese zodiac signs that originally appeared during one's birth year appears once again. They became special birthdays because in the past not many babies made it to their 돌 and not many people lived up to sixty-one years.

An interesting tradition of 돌 is 돌잡이. Items such as money, rice, books, pencils, thread, a microphone, and so on are arranged on a table for the baby to pick up. It is believed that the item which the baby picks foretells the baby's future. Money and rice are interpreted as symbols of a wealthy life, books and pencils as academic success, thread as a long and healthy life, and the microphone as a promising career in the entertainment business. On 환갑, children honor their parents with a large feast and much merrymaking. Close relatives are also invited to join in the festivities to show their respect and to give presents.

Conversation 2   할머니 연세가 어떻게 되세요?

Conversation   2

마크: 제니 씨, 주말에 바빴어요?

제니: 네, 일요일이 할머니 생신[G9.3]이었어요.

그래서 가족들하고 같이 저녁을 먹었어요.

마크: 아, 그랬어요?

제니: 네, 오래간만에 즐거운 시간을 보냈어요.

마크: 할머니께 무슨 선물 드렸어요?

제니: 스웨터하고 장갑을 드렸어요.

할머니께서 아주 좋아하셨어요.[G9.4]

마크: 할머니 연세가 어떻게 되세요?

제니: 올해 일흔 다섯이세요.

마크: 할머니께서 건강하세요?

제니: 네, 연세는 많으시지만[G9.5] 아주 건강하세요.

NEW WORDS

NOUN

가족	family
나이	age
딸	daughter
댁 *hon.*	home, house (=집 *plain*)
사진	photo, picture
생신 *hon.*	birthday (=생일 *plain*)
성함 *hon.*	name (=이름 *plain*)
스웨터	sweater
아들	son
연세 *hon.*	age (=나이 *plain*)
작년	last year
장갑	gloves
할머니	grandmother
할아버지	grandfather

COUNTER

살	years old
분 *hon.*	people (=명 *plain*)

VERB

돌아가시다 *hon.*	to pass away (=죽다 *plain*)
드리다 *hum.*	to give (=주다 *plain*)
드시다 *hon.*	to eat (=먹다 *plain*)
주무시다 *hon.*	to sleep (=자다 *plain*)
죽다	to die
찍다	to take (a photo)

ADJECTIVE

건강하다	to be healthy
즐겁다	to be joyful

ADVERB

모두	all

PARTICLE

께서 *hon.*	subject particle (=이/가 *plain*)

SUFFIX

~(으)시	subject honorific
~지만	clausal connective

NEW EXPRESSIONS

1. 께 is the honorific counterpart of 한테. It is used for highly respected seniors: for example, parents, grandparents, or teachers.

2. 께서 is the honorific counterpart of the subject particle 이/가, not of 한테서 'from (a person)'. The honorific form of 한테서 is also 께 as in 부모님께 편지를 받았어요.

3. 보내다 'to send' has an additional meaning, 'to spend time', as in 가족들하고 즐거운 시간을 보냈어요 (Lesson 7, Conv. 2).

4. 어떻게 되세요? is a polite idiomatic expression that is the equivalent to 뭐예요? 언제예요? 몇이에요? (what is . . . , when is . . . , how many/much is . . .). For example, it would be more appropriate to use the expression 성함이 어떻게 되세요? than 이름이 뭐예요? when addressing seniors or new acquaintances.

Exercise

Connect the corresponding words.

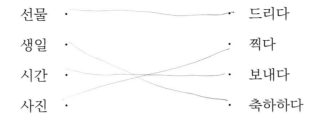

선물 ·   · 드리다

생일 ·   · 찍다

시간 ·   · 보내다

사진 ·   · 축하하다

Grammar

G9.3   Honorific expressions

Examples

(1)   동생이 책을 읽어요.   My younger sibling is reading
                                     a book.

      아버지**께서** 책을 읽**으세**요.   My father is reading a book.
                                     (subject honorific)

(2)   제 동생 나이는 열 여덟 살이에요.   My younger sibling is 18
                                     years old.

      저희 할머니 **연세**는   My grandmother is 72 years
      일흔 둘**이세**요.   old. **(subject honorific)**

(3)   우리 집 개는 작년에 죽었습니다.
      저희 할아버지**께서** 작년에 **돌아가셨**습니다.

Notes

Korean is a language whose honorific patterns are highly systematic. Honorific
forms appear in hierarchical address/reference terms and titles, some
commonly used nouns and verbs, the pronoun system, particles, and verb
suffixes. Sentences in Korean can hardly be composed without knowledge of
one's social relationships to the listener or referent in terms of age, social status,
and kinship. The following table is a summary of honorific forms.

		Plain	Honorific	Humble
Nouns	age	나이	연세	
	name	이름	성함	
	birthday	생일	생신	
	words	말	말씀	
	house	집	댁	
	meal	밥	진지	
	counter for people	사람/명	분	
Pronouns	he/she	이/그/저 사람	이/그/저 분	
	I	나는/내가		저는/제가
	my	내		제
	we/our	우리		저희
Verbs	to see/meet someone	보다/만나다	보시다/만나시다	뵙다
	to be/to have	있다	계시다/있으시다	
	to die	죽다	돌아가시다	
	to be well, fine	잘 있다	안녕하시다	
	to sleep	자다	주무시다	
	to eat	먹다	잡수시다/드시다	
	to give	주다	주시다	드리다
	to speak	말하다	말씀하시다	말씀드리다
Particles	subject	이/가	께서	
	topic	은/는	께서는	
	goal	한테/에게	께	
	source	한테서/에게서	께	
Suffixes	professor	교수	교수님	
	parents	부모	부모님	
	teacher	선생	선생님	

Subject honorific forms: [N께서 . . . V/Adj~(으)시]

The particle 께서 is the honorific counterpart of the subject particle 이/가. The subject honorific suffix ~(으)시 is used when the subject—a social or familial superior, a distant peer, or a stranger—must be referred to or spoken to with respect.

While ~(으)시 must be used when the subject is honored, use of 께서 is not obligatory. When it is used, it shows special respect toward the subject of the sentence.

내 동생이 도서관에 가요.   vs.   저희 할머니께서 집에 가세요.

When talking about your grandparents, parents, or any elders, the subject honorific particle 께서 is used in addition to the subject honorific suffix ~(으)시 to pay respect to them. When talking about your close friends or younger siblings, on the other hand, ~(으)시 is not allowed. Note further that the presence of ~어요/아요 or ~습/ㅂ니다 shows respect to the listener.

Some nouns and verbs have honorific counterparts such as 나이/연세, 이름/성함, 딸 /따님, 아들 /아드님, 자다/주무시다, 먹다/드시다, as shown in the following example sentences.

할아버지께서는 연세가 많으세요. My grandfather is old.
                                     (*lit.* My grandfather has much age.)

선생님, 따님은 어디에 계세요?   Sir, where is your daughter?

아버지께서 지금 주무십니다.   My father is sleeping now.

Exercise

Choose the appropriate forms within the [ ] and circle them.

(1) Server: [모두 몇 분이세요?/모두 몇 사람이에요?]
     Customer: [세 분이에요./세 사람이에요.]
(2) 할머니께서 동생한테 책을 [주었어요/주셨어요/드렸어요.]
(3) 저희 부모님께서는 [연세가 많으세요/나이가 많으세요.]
(4) 아버지, 저 약국에 [갑니다/가십니다/가실 거예요.]
(5) 할아버지, 저기 동생이 [와요/오세요/오십니다.]

G9.4 The subject honorific ~(으)시

(1) 마이클: 어, 제니 씨. 요즘 어떻게 지내**세**요?

제니: 잘 지내요. 마이클 씨, 이번 학기에도 심리학 들**으세**요?

마이클: 아니요, 이번 학기에는 안 들어요.

(2) 마크: 스티브 씨 어디서 오**셨**어요?

스티브: 저는 미국 보스턴에서 왔어요.

(3) 마크: 저어, 이번 학기에 한국어를 누가 가르치**십**니까?

현우: 이민수 선생님께서 가르치**십**니다.

(4) 마크: 이민수 선생님 계**십**니까?

현우: 지금 안 **계세**요.

Notes

1. ~(으)시 is added to a predicate stem to express the speaker's respect toward the subject of the sentence.

2. ~(으)시 is not a sentence-final suffix, and therefore it is always followed by other types of suffixes as in 읽으시었습니다 [읽+으시+었+습니다].

	Plain		Subject honorific	
	Non-past	Past	Non-past	Past
Polite	~어/아요	~었/았어요	~(으)세요	~(으)셨어요
Deferential	~(스)ㅂ니다	~었/았습니다	~(으)십니다	~(으)셨습니다

Examples

	Plain		Subject Honorific	
	Non-past	Past	Non-past	Past
Polite	가요 읽어요	갔어요 읽었어요	가세요 읽으세요	가셨어요 읽으셨어요
Deferential	갑니다 읽습니다	갔습니다 읽었습니다	가십니다 읽으십니다	가셨습니다 읽으셨습니다

3. ~(으)시 is already part of some honorific predicates, as in example (4).

	Non-past	Past
Polite	계세요	계셨어요
Deferential	계십니다	계셨습니다

Exercise

Fill in the blanks with appropriate honorific forms of the verb. Be consistent with the tense and the speech style in the conversation.

(1) 마크: 스티브 씨, 어디서 <u>오셨어요</u> (오다)?

스티브: 저는 미국 보스턴에서 왔어요.

(2) A: 김 선생님 _____ (계시다)?

B: 지금 안 _____ (계시다).

수업에 _____ (가다).

(3) A: 이 지도 어느 서점에서 _____ (사다)?

B: 동네 서점에서 샀어요.

(4) 마크: 선생님, 점심 _____ (드시다)?

선생님: 아니요, 아직 안 먹었어요.

(5) 지난 학기에 몇 과목 _____ (듣다)?

이번 학기에는 몇 과목 _____ (듣다)?

다음 학기에는 몇 과목 _____ (듣다)?

G9.5   The clausal connective ~지만

(1) 저는 여행은 자주 하**지만**   I travel often but don't take
     사진은 안 찍어요.   pictures.

(2) 나는 편지를 자주 쓰**지만**   I write letters often,
     내 친구는 자주 안 써요.   but my friend does not.

(3) A: 테니스 좋아하세요?
     B: 좋아하**지만** 자주 못 쳐요.

 Notes

1. ~지만 is equivalent to "but" or "although" in English. Remember that with ~고 it is more natural not to express tense in the first clause, but to rely on the second clause to furnish it. This is not the case with ~지만, where both clauses in the sentence must indicate the tense. For example:

쇼핑을 하고 친구를 만났어요.   (no tense indicated in first clause)
생일 파티에는 못 **갔**지만 선물은 샀어요.   (tense indicated in first clause)

Exercises

1. Connect the clauses in each sentence using the ending ~지만. Change the verb to the past tense if necessary.

(1) 이 시계는 조금 (비싸다) <u>비싸지만</u> 아주 좋아요.
(2) 미국은 겨울 방학은 (짧다) _____ 여름 방학은 길어요.
(3) 공부는 (하다) _____ 시험을 못 봤어요.
(4) 마크는 어제 (바쁘다) _____ 친구 파티에 갔어요.
(5) 다음 월요일이 크리스마스(이다) _____ 일을 해요.
(6) 형은 한국에서 (살다) _____ 저는 미국에서 살아요.

2. Use ~지만 to make a complex sentence by changing the verb and adding an appropriate main clause as in the example.

    (1)   한국은 날씨가 참 좋아요.

         <u>한국은 날씨가 참 좋지만 겨울이 좀 추워요.</u>

    (2)   주말이 좋아요.

         _____

    (3)   내 여동생은 전공이 없어요.

         _____

    (4)   우리 가족은 미국에서 살아요.

         _____

    (5)   서울에는 사람이 아주 많아요.

         _____

    (6)   작년 크리스마스에는 선물을 많이 받았어요.

         _____

Notes

Narration	돌잔치

지난 토요일이 한국어 선생님 딸 돌이었습니다. 그래서 저는 반 친구들하고 같이 선생님 댁에 갔습니다. 한국에서는 한 살에 돌잔치[1]를 합니다. 보통 돌잔치에서는 재미있는 일[2]들이 많습니다. 테이블 위에 돈, 연필, 실[3]을 놓습니다. 돈은 부자[4]를 뜻하고[5] 연필은 공부를 뜻하고 실은 건강을 뜻합니다. 선생님 딸은 연필을 잡았습니다[6].
우리는 맛있는 음식도 많이 먹고 사진도 많이 찍었습니다.
즐거운 돌잔치였습니다.

1. 잔치: party, feast
2. 일: event
3. 실: thread
4. 부자: a wealthy person
5. 뜻하다: to mean, to signify
6. 잡다: to catch, to grab

Exercises

1. Read the narration and answer the following questions using the deferential ending ~(스)ㅂ니다.

    (1) 돌잔치는 무엇입니까?

    (2) 누구의 돌잔치가 있었습니까?

    (3) 돌잔치에 누구하고 같이 갔습니까?

    (3) 실과 돈은 무엇을 뜻합니까?

    (5) 한국의 돌잔치는 뭐가 재미있습니까?

    (6) 선생님 딸은 돌잔치에서 무엇을 잡았습니까?

2. Fill in the blanks with the appropriate words from the box below.

맛있는	큰	많이	재미있는
같이	그래서	지난	즐거운

한국에서는 한 살에 돌잔치를 합니다. _지난_ 토요일이 한국어 선생님 딸 돌이었습니다. _그래서_ 저는 반 친구들하고 _같이_ 선생님 댁에 갔습니다. 돌잔치에서 _재미있는_ 일이 많았습니다. 테이블 위에 돈, 연필, 실이 있었습니다. 돈은 부자를 뜻하고 연필은 공부를 뜻하고 실은 건강을 뜻합니다. 선생님 딸은 연필을 잡았습니다. _맛있는_ 음식도 많이 먹고 사진도 _많이_ 찍었습니다. _즐거운_ 돌잔치였습니다.

USAGE

A Talking about important dates

Exercise

Ask your partner about the following dates.

   (1) today A: 오늘이 며칠이에요?
               B: <u>오늘은 12월 12일이에요.</u>
   (2) your partner's birthday
   (3) Valentine's Day
   (4) Independence Day
   (5) Thanksgiving
   (6) Christmas

B Dates, days, and schedules

December 2020

일요일	월요일	화요일	수요일	목요일	금요일	토요일
	3:00 p.m. 한국어 랩 1	2	Today 3	4	5	3:30 p.m. 농구시합: _____ vs. UCLA 6
7	3:00 p.m. 한국어 랩 8	9:00 a.m. 한국어 복습 9	10	9:00 a.m. 한국어 오럴테스트 11	12	1:30 p.m. 농구시합: _____ vs. Michigan 13
14	8–10 a.m. 한국어 Final exam 15	16	12:30 p.m. 경제학 Final exam 17	Semester ends 18	19	20
21	22	23	24	*Christmas Day* 25	26	11:00 a.m. to Boston 27

(1) 오늘은 며칠이에요?   오늘은 12월 3일이에요.

(2) 한국어 랩은 무슨 요일에 있어요? 몇 시에 있어요?

(3) 한국어 복습('review')은 언제 해요?

(4) 15일에는 무슨 시험이 있어요? 시험이 몇 시간 걸려요?

(5) 다음 주에는 누가 농구시합('basketball game')을 해요?
몇 시에 해요?

(6) 경제학 시험은 언제예요?

(7) 이번 학기는 며칠에 끝나요('to end')?

(8) 보스턴에는 언제 가요?

(9) 올해 크리스마스는 무슨 요일이에요?

(10) 내년은 몇 년이에요?

C *Giving/making/sending and receiving*

giving or sending	receiving
N한테 선물(을) 하다/주다/드리다	N한테서 선물(을) 받다
N한테 전화(를) 하다/걸다/드리다	N한테서 전화(를) 받다
N한테 편지(를) 하다/쓰다/보내다	N한테서 편지(를) 받다
N한테 이메일(을) 하다/보내다	N한테서 이메일(을) 받다

 Exercise

Give a description in answer to the following questions.

(1) 생일에 무슨 선물을 받았어요?

(2) 이번 토요일이 친구 생일이에요. 무슨 선물을 줄 거예요?

(3) 누구한테 자주 전화하세요?

(4) 선생님께 언제 전화 드렸어요?

(5) 부모님께 언제 전화 받았어요?

(6) 누구한테 크리스마스 카드를 보낼 거예요?

(7) 작년에 누구한테서 크리스마스 카드를 받았어요?

(8) 부모님께 편지 자주 쓰세요?

D   *Organizing a birthday party*

 Exercise

You are organizing a birthday party. Form groups of three or four. Each group prepares for the birthday party of one of their own. Include some of the following:

(1)   Whose birthday it is

(2)   Date, time, and place of the party

(3)   What to include in the invitation

(4)   Deciding on birthday presents

(5)   Things to bring for the party

(6)   Sending out thank-you notes

Notes

....

....

....

....

....

....

Lesson 9 Birthday

CONVERSATION 1 *I received a pretty hat for a present.*

Steve:	Lisa, what did you do last weekend?
Lisa:	Saturday was my birthday, so I had a birthday party.
Steve:	Oh, really? Congratulations!
Lisa:	Thank you.
Steve:	Did you receive a lot of birthday presents?
Lisa:	Yes, I received a lot from my friends.[G9.1]
Steve:	What kinds of presents did you receive?
Lisa:	I received a pretty hat and a book.[G9.2]
	When is your birthday, Steve?
Steve:	My birthday is June 27th.

CONVERSATION 2   *How old is your grandmother?*

Mark:	Jenny, were you busy on the weekend?
Jenny:	Yes, Sunday was my grandmother's birthday[G9.3] so I ate dinner with my family.
Mark:	Oh, really?
Jenny:	Yes, I had some fun for the first time in a while.
Mark:	What kind of present did you give to your grandmother?
Jenny:	I gave her a sweater and gloves.
	My grandmother liked them very much.[G9.4]
Mark:	How old is your grandmother?
Jenny:	She's seventy-five this year.
Mark:	Is your grandmother in good health?
Jenny:	Yes, she's elderly but very healthy.[G9.5]

NARRATION   *First-birthday party*

Last Saturday was my Korean teacher's daughter's first birthday, so I went to my teacher's house with my classmates. In Korea, they have first-birthday parties at the age of one. Usually, there are lots of fun things to do at first-birthday parties. Money, a pencil, and some thread are placed on the table. The money represents wealth, the pencil represents studies, and the thread represents health. My teacher's daughter grabbed the pencil. We ate a lot of delicious food and also took a lot of pictures. It was a fun first-birthday party.

10과 연구실에서

Lesson 10 At a Professor's Office

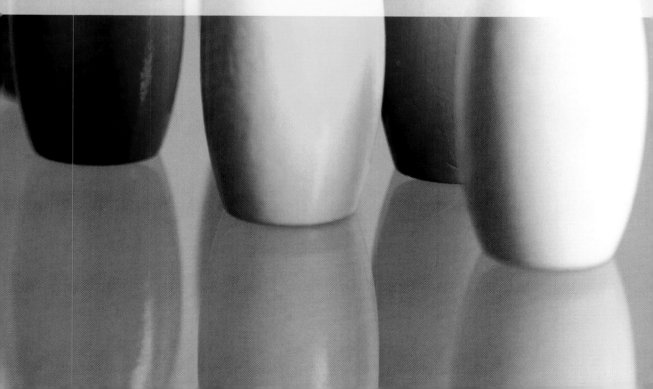

Conversation 1   오늘은 시간이 없는데요.

▌ Mark introduces himself to Professor Park and makes an arrangement to
take the Korean placement test.

Conversation   1

마크: 안녕하세요, 교수님.

교수님: 네, 어떻게 오셨어요?

마크: 제 이름은 마크 스미스입니다.

          한국 문화를 전공하는데$^{G10.1}$ 이번 학기에

          한국어 수업을 듣고 싶습니다.$^{G10.2}$

교수님: 아, 그래요? 한국어를 얼마 동안 배웠어요?

마크: 시드니 대학교에서 일 년 동안 배웠습니다.

교수님: 그럼 오늘 오후에 한국어 시험을 보세요.

마크: 죄송하지만 오늘은 시간이 없는데요.$^{G10.3}$

교수님: 그럼 내일 아침 9시에 시험을 보러 오세요.

마크: 네. 그럼 내일 뵙겠습니다.

NEW WORDS

NOUN		ADJECTIVE	
교수	professor	싶다	to want to
동안	during, for	죄송하다	to be sorry
문화	culture	**ADVERB**	
밖	outside	그냥	just, without any special reason
시드니	Sydney		
연구실	professor's office	굉장히	very much
택시	taxi	일찍	early
호주	Australia	**SUFFIX**	
VERB		~(으)ㄴ데/는데	clausal connective
놀다	to play; to not work	~(으)ㄴ데요/	a polite sentence ending for background information
시작하다	to begin	는데요	

NEW EXPRESSIONS

1. 얼마 'how much', when used with 동안 'during' as in 얼마 동안, means 'for how long'. 동안 in 일 년 동안 'for one year' and 여름 방학 동안 'during the summer break' indicates a duration or period of time. 동안 can be omitted in some contexts, as in 한국어를 일 년 (동안) 배웠습니다 'I studied Korean for one year'.

2. A: 전공이 뭐예요? / 뭐 전공하세요?   What is your major?
    B: 심리학이에요. /   I major in psychology.
    심리학을 전공해요.

3. The verb 뵙다 in 내일 뵙겠습니다 'I will see you tomorrow' is the humble form of the verb 보다 'to see' (see G9.3).

Exercises

1. Complete the words by filling in the blanks.

oriental studies: (동양)학		economics: ( )학	
biology: ( )학		Korean studies: ( )학	
psychology: ( )학		political science: ( )학	

2. Ask your classmates the following questions.

A: (한국어, 일본어, 중국어, 테니스, 수영) 얼마 동안 배웠어요?

B: _____ 동안 배웠어요.

Grammar

G10.1   The clausal connective ~(으)ㄴ데/는데

Examples

(1)   어제 샌디한테 전화**했는데**
      집에 없었어요.

I called Sandy yesterday,
but she was not home.

(2)   A: 날씨가 좋**은데**
          집에 있을 거예요?
      B: 네, 집에 있을 거예요.

The weather is nice; are you
going to stay at home?
Yes, I'm going to stay at home.

(3)   옷이 예**쁜데** 너무 비싸요.

The clothes are pretty but
too expensive.

(4)   시간이 없**는데** 택시를 타세요.

You are running out of time;
take a taxi.

Notes

1. The main function of ~(으)ㄴ데/는데 is to provide background information about the situation in the main clause. The pattern ~(으)ㄴ데/는데 can be used in the following contexts:

  a.   to give common background information to be shared between a speaker and a listener (examples (1) and (2));

  b.   to contrast two clauses (example (3));

  c.   to justify a request or proposal (example (4)).

2. ~(으)ㄴ데 and ~는데 alternate as follows:

~(으)ㄴ데		~는데	
a.	Adjectives	c.	Verbs
b.	Copula	d.	Past tense
		e.	Existential 있/없

In the past tense, ~었/았 occurs before the form ~는데. The following table shows the conjugation patterns.

The suffix ~(으)ㄴ데

a. Adjectives

Dictionary form		Non-past	Past
예쁘다	to be pretty	예쁜데	예뻤는데
좋다	to be good	좋은데	좋았는데
멀다	to be far	먼데	멀었는데
춥다	to be cold	추운데	추웠는데

b. The copula N~이다, N(이)아니다

Dictionary form	Non-past	Past
학생이다 to be a student	학생인데	학생이었는데
교수이다 to be a professor	교수인데	교수였는데
학생(이) 아니다 to not be . . .	학생(이) 아닌데	학생(이) 아니었는데

The suffix ~는데

c–d. Verbs/Past tense

Dictionary form		Non-past	Past
가다	to go	가는데	갔는데
먹다	to eat	먹는데	먹었는데
알다	to know	아는데	알았는데
듣다	to listen	듣는데	들었는데

e. 있다/없다

Dictionary form		Non-past	Past
있다	to be, exist	있는데	있었는데
없다	to not be, not exist	없는데	없었는데

Exercise

Combine each pair of sentences using the correct form of ~(으)ㄴ데/는데.

(1) 한국어를 (배워요). <u>배우는데</u> 재미있어요.

(2) 마크는 호주 사람(이에요). _____ 한국어를 굉장히 잘 해요.

(3) 경제학 수업은 재미(있어요). _____ 숙제가 많아요.

(4) 기숙사에 (살아요). _____ 방이 좁아요.

(5) 어제 공부 많이 (했어요). _____ 오늘 시험이 없어요.

(6) 우리 학교 캠퍼스는 (예뻐요). _____너무 작아요.

G10.2   Expressing desire: ~고 싶다/ 고 싶어 하다

(1) 마크: 이번 주말에 뭐 하**고 싶어요**?   What do you want to do this weekend?

스티브: 수영하러 가**고 싶어요**.   I want to go swimming.

(2) 유미는 한국 영화를 보**고 싶어 해요**.   Yumi wants to watch a Korean movie.

(3) A: 내일 어디 가**고 싶으세요**?   Where do you want to go tomorrow?

B: 그냥 집에 있**고 싶어요**.   I just want to stay home.

(4) 올해에는 운동을 시작하**고 싶었는데** 못 했어요.

Examples

Notes

Verb~고 싶다 expresses the speaker's desire or, in questions, the listener's desire. The desire or wish of a third person is indicated by ~고 싶어 하다 (*lit.* someone shows signs of wanting).

저는 컴퓨터를 사고 싶어요.	I want to buy a computer.
소피아도 컴퓨터를 사고 싶어 해요.	Sophia also wants to buy a computer.

The past-tense form of ~고 싶어요 is not ~었/았고 싶어요 but ~고 싶었어요.

집에 일찍 가고 싶어요.	I want to go home early.
집에 일찍 가고 싶었어요.	I wanted to go home early.

Exercises

1. Ask your partner these questions.

    (1) 저녁에 뭐 먹고 싶으세요?

    (2) 이번 주말에 뭐 하고 싶어요?

    (3) 방학에 어디 가고 싶으세요?

    (4) 생일에 무슨 선물을 받고 싶으세요?

    (5) 무슨 차를 타고 싶으세요?

2. Change the following sentences as in the example.

    (1) 제니 / 옷 / 사다   제니는 옷을 사고 싶어 해요.

    (2) 마크 / 테니스 / 치다   _____

    (3) 저 / 한국 음식 / 먹다   _____

    (4) 린다 / 한국 노래 / 배우다   _____

    (5) 유미 / 책 / 사다   _____

    (6) 나 / 친구 / 만나다   _____

    (7) 김 선생님 / 영화 / 보다   _____

G10.3   The sentence ending ~(으)ㄴ데요/는데요

Examples

(1) A: 여기가 김 교수님 연구실이지요?

B: 네, 그런**데요**.

A: 김 교수님 지금 계세요?

B: 지금 안 계시**는데요**.   He is not here now.

(2) A: 날씨가 좋은데 밖에 놀러 가요.   The weather is nice;
                                        let's go out to play.

B: 미안해요. 약속이 있**는데요**.   I'm sorry. I have a
                                        prior engagement.

 Notes

1. The sentence ending ~(으)ㄴ데요/는데요 is an extended usage of the clausal connective ~(으)ㄴ데/는데 (G10.1). By using ~(으)ㄴ데요/는데요, the speaker presents background information and lets the listener figure out what to do. Thus, it may be used as an expression of politeness. For example, in (1) above speaker B uses 안 계시는데요 to respond instead of 안 계세요, so that speaker A can figure out what to do next. "Would you like to leave a message?" or "Can I do anything for you?" is implied.

2. Compare the use of ~어요/아요 and of ~(으)ㄴ데요/는데요 in the following telephone dialogue:

A: 마크 씨 집에 있어요?   Is Mark home?

B: a. 지금 없어요.   He is not at home.
                                 (direct/assertive)

     b. 지금 없는데요.   He is not at home. (Is there
                                 anything I can do for you?)
                                 (indirect)

2. The ~(으)ㄴ데요/는데요 form is also used to deal with delicate situations such as disagreement, denial, and rejection. For instance, speaker B in (2) above avoids a direct rejection by conveying his situation implicitly. The ~(으)ㄴ데요/는데요 form allows speakers to avoid explicitly stating their intentions.

Exercise

Respond to the following sentences using the ~(으)ㄴ데요/는데요 form to express disagreement, denial, or rejection.

(1) 시간 좀 있으세요?   <u>지금은 시간 없는데요.</u>

(2) 내일 파티에 같이 가요.   _____

(3) 박 교수님 지금 계세요?   _____

(4) 오늘 시험이 어땠어요?   _____

(5) 이 식당 음식이 맛있지요?   _____

(6) 같이 공원에 놀러 가요.   _____

Notes

· ·

· ·

· ·

· ·

· ·

· ·

Conversation 2   늦어서 죄송합니다.

▌ Mark is late for the Korean placement test.

Conversation 2

(똑똑)

교수님: 네, 들어오세요.

마크: 늦어서[G10.4] 죄송합니다.

차가 많이 막혀서 늦었습니다.

교수님: 서울 교통이 무척 복잡하지요? 뭐 타고 왔어요?

마크: 여기까지 직접 오는[G10.5] 버스가 없어서

택시를 타고 왔어요.

교수님: 택시도 괜찮지만 다음부터는 지하철을 타세요.

지하철이 빠르고 편해요.

마크: 여기 오는 지하철은 몇 호선이에요?

교수님: 2호선이에요.

NEW WORDS

NOUN

가수	singer
교통	transportation; traffic
날	day
머리	① head;
	② hair
일	④ event

ADVERB

다음부터(는)	from next time
무척	very much
직접	directly

SUFFIX

~어서/아서	clausal connective (cause)
~는	noun-modifying form (verb)

VERB

늦다	to be late
들어오다	to come in
이사하다	to move

ADJECTIVE

막히다	to be blocked, congested
복잡하다	to be crowded
불편하다	to be uncomfortable, inconvenient
빠르다	to be fast
아프다	to be sick
편하다	to be comfortable, convenient

CONJUNCTION

그렇지만	but, however

NEW EXPRESSIONS

1. 죄송합니다 'I am very sorry' literally means 'I feel guilty'. This expression is appropriate in speaking to a person of higher status. 미안합니다 'I am sorry' (*lit.* I feel uncomfortable) is usually used to a peer.

2. 교통이 복잡하지요? 'Traffic is congested, isn't it?' literally means 'Traffic is complicated, isn't it?' 교통 alone means 'transportation', not 'traffic'.

3. 똑똑 expresses a door knocking sound equivalent to "knock knock."

Exercises

1. Fill in the blanks with appropriate verbs or adjectives.

   (1) 서울에는 차가 아주 많아요. 그래서 교통이 ~~복잡해요~~ 복잡해요.

   (2) 오늘 아침 9시 30분에 일어났어요. 그래서 10시 한국어
       수업에 _____.

   (3) 택시는 _____. 그렇지만 너무 비싸요.

   (4) 보통 오후 6시에는 차가 많이 _____.

2. Ask your classmates the following questions.

   (1) 동네/학교 근처 교통이 어때요?

   (2) 학교에 어떻게 오세요?

   (3) 왜 자전거/버스/지하철/차를 타고 오세요?
       (or 왜 걸어서 오세요?)

/   **Notes**

Grammar

G10.4   The clausal connective ~어서/아서 (cause)

Examples

(1) A: 왜 한국어를 배우세요?   Why do you study
                                          Korean?

     B: **재미있어서** 배워요.   It's fun, so I am
                                          learning it.

     C: 한국어를 잘 하고 **싶어서** 배워요.   I want to speak
                                          Korean well,
                                          so I learn.

(2) A: 오늘 아침 수업에 왜 늦었어요?
     B: 일이 **있어서** 늦었어요.

(3) 어제 머리가 **아파서** 타이레놀을 먹었어요.

(4) 집 근처에 마켓이 **없어서** 불편해요.

Some fixed uses of ~어서/아서:

(5) **늦어서** 죄송합니다.   I'm sorry for being
                                       late.

(6) 전화 **주셔서** 감사합니다/고맙습니다.   Thank you very much
                                       for giving me a call.

Notes

1. The pattern [Clause 1~어서/아서 + Clause 2] is used to give a cause or reason for the event described in Clause 2. Because [Clause 1~어서/아서] expresses a reason or a cause, it is often used in response to the question 왜 'Why', as in examples (1) and (2).

2. Note that there is a close temporal relation between the two events in example (3). That is, the event in Clause 2 (taking some Tylenol) cannot take place before the event in Clause 1 (having a headache).

3. The choice between ~어서 and ~아서 is determined by the same principle that determines the choice between ~어요 and ~아요 as in the table provided below.

Dictionary form	~어요/아요	~어서/아서
좋다	좋아요	좋아서
아프다	아파요	아파서
늦다	늦어요	늦어서
재미있다	재미있어요	재미있어서
복잡하다	복잡해요	복잡해서
가깝다	가까워요	가까워서

4. In example (3), ~어서/아서 in the first clause never takes a tense marker. For example, unlike English, the past-tense suffix cannot occur in 머리가 아파서 (Clause 1) even though the tense of the main clause (Clause 2) is past, as in 타이레놀을 먹었어요.

5. The main clause (Clause 2) may be omitted if the context makes it clear to the listener what is omitted. The polite ending ~요 should be attached to maintain the polite speech level.

> A:　　왜 한국어를 배우세요? Why are you learning Korean?
>
> B:　　한국에 가고 **싶어서**요. Because I want to go to Korea.

Exercises

1. Practice as in the example.

  (1) 오후에 수업이 없다 / 테니스를 치다

      오후에 수업이 **없어서** 테니스를 쳐요.

  (2) 날씨가 덥다 / 수영하다

      _____

  (3) 교통이 복잡하다 / 지하철로 학교에 가다

      _____

  (4) 한국어를 배우고 싶다 / 서울에 가다

      _____

  (5) 집에서 마켓까지 가깝다 / 걸어서 가다

      _____

  (6) 날씨가 춥다 / 그냥 집에 있다

      _____

2. Answer the following questions using ~어서/아서.

  (1) 왜 이 수업을 들어요?   _____

  (2) 오늘 왜 수업에 늦었어요? _____

  (3) 어제 왜 학교에 안 왔어요? _____

Notes

G10.5   The noun-modifying form [Verb~는] +N

(1) 한국어를 **배우는** 학생들이 많아요.　There are many students who learn Korean.

(2) 수업 **없는** 날은 뭐하세요?

(3) 기숙사에 **사는** 사람이 누구예요?　Who is the person who lives in the dormitory?

(4) A: 테니스 잘 **치는** 사람을 아세요?　Do you know a person who plays tennis well?

　　B: 제 친구**인** 스티브가 잘 쳐요.　Steve, who is my friend, plays well.

(5) 제가 보고 **싶은** 영화는 '괴물'이에요.　The movie that I want to watch is *The Host*.

❖   Notes

1. A construction consisting of [Adj/Verb~(으)ㄴ/는] + N is called a relative clause. It is a type of noun-modifying construction. Compare the word order of a noun-modifying construction in English and Korean.

English:　The newspaper　that I read　is *Times*.
　　　　　　　a　　　　　　　b　　　　　c

Korean:　내가 읽는　신문은　타임스예요.
　　　　　　b　　　　a　　　　c

As shown above, relative clauses in Korean have the following characteristics:

a.　　In Korean, the modifying clause 내가 읽는 'that I read' precedes the modified noun 신문 'the newspaper', whereas in English the modifying clause 'that I read' follows the modified noun 'the newspaper'.

b. In Korean, there are no relative pronouns such as 'which', 'who', and 'that' as in English.

c. The topic marker 은/는 cannot occur in a relative clause. 이/가 is used instead: 내가 읽는 책 'the book that I read', not 나는 읽는 책.

2. For /ㄹ/ irregular verbs, the stem-final /ㄹ/ is deleted before ~는 or ~시.

Dictionary form		~는 form	~(으)시는 honorific form
살다	to live	사는	사시는
만들다	to make	만드는	만드시는
알다	to know	아는	아시는

기숙사에 사는 학생   a student who lives in the dorm
음식을 만드시는 어머니   a mother who makes food
잘 아는 사이   a relationship where they know (each other) well

Note that the adjectives 멀다 and 길다 become 먼 and 긴.

3. 있다/없다 (e.g., 맛있다/맛없다) occurs with ~는 like any other verbs when the relative clause is in the present tense (G9.2).

책상 위에 있는 게 뭐예요?   What is that thing that is on the desk?

수업이 없는 날 뭐 하세요?   What do you do on the days that you don't have classes?

4. The copula ~(이)다/아니다 becomes ~인/아닌 or ~이신/아니신 for noun-modifying forms.

고등학생인 내 동생은 지금 도서관에서 공부해요.   My younger sibling, who is a high school student, is studying at the library now.

의사이신 우리 아버지를 만나세요.   Meet my father, who is a medical doctor.

학생 아닌 사람은 수업을 못 들어요.   Those who are not students cannot take classes.

5. As noted in G9.2, adjectives take the ~(으)ㄴ form as in 큰 (크다), 예쁜 (예쁘다), 먼 (멀다) and the desirative auxiliary adjective ~고 싶다 takes the ~(으)ㄴ form as in ~고 싶은.

저는 키('height')가 커요. 그렇지만 키가 작은 사람을 좋아해요.
제가 먹고 싶은 음식은 햄버거예요.

Exercises

1. Draw a square around the noun-modifying phrase, and circle the modified noun in each sentence. Then, translate the sentence into English.

(1) 신문을 읽으시는 분은 우리 어머니세요.
     The person who is reading the newspaper is my mother.

(2) 여기가 제가 사는 동네예요.
     _____

(3) 이건 마이클이 자주 듣는 노래예요.
     _____

(4) 방에 계시는 분은 우리 할머니세요.
     _____

(5) 저는 김 선생님이 가르치시는 수업을 들어요.
     _____

(6) 민지가 이사하는 집이 여기서 멀어요?
     _____

2. Describe the following nouns, using the construction [Verb~는] + N.

(1) 가수   가수는 [노래를 하는] **사람**이에요.
(2) 학생   _____
(3) 룸메이트   _____
(4) 선생님   _____

Narration 호주 학생 마크

저는 호주 사람입니다. 한국어와 한국 문화를 배우고 싶어서 지난 달에 서울에 왔습니다. 호주에서 일 년 동안 한국어를 배웠습니다. 호주에는 한국어를 가르치는 학교가 많이 있습니다. 저는 이번 학기에 서울대학교 대학원에서 한국 문화를 전공합니다. 그리고 박 교수님이 가르치시는 한국어 수업도 듣습니다. 지난 달에 박 교수님 연구실에서 한국어 시험을 봤습니다. 그런데 차가 많이 막혀서 10분 늦었습니다. 서울은 교통이 무척 복잡하고 사람들이 굉장히 많습니다. 교통이 불편해서 저는 다음 주에 학교 기숙사로 이사합니다. 그렇지만 재미있는 일들도 많이 있습니다.

Exercises

1. Read the narration and answer the following questions.

    (1) 마크는 어디에서 왔습니까?
    (2) 왜 서울에 왔습니까?
    (3) 마크는 어디에서 무슨 공부를 합니까?
    (4) 마크는 무슨 시험을 봤습니까? 왜 봤습니까?
    (5) 마크는 왜 시험에 늦었습니까?
    (6) 서울의 교통은 어떻습니까?
    (7) 마크는 언제, 왜 기숙사로 이사합니까?

2. Retell the story in the narration to your partner using your own words.

3. Now, summarize the narration in your own words using 5–6 sentences.

CULTURE

아름다운 한복 (Beautiful *hanbok*)

한복 is a term collectively used for traditional Korean clothes. These are often characterized as a set of colorful garments with simple lines that don't have any pockets. Although 한복 literally means "Korean clothing," 한복 today particularly refers to the clothing of the Joseon dynasty. Typically, women wear a wraparound skirt (치마) and men wear roomy pants bound at the ankle (바지). 저고리, an upper garment with a ribbon to tie in the front, was worn by both women and men. With the developments in textiles as well as changes in society, a wide selection of fabrics became available to make 한복—from ramie and cotton to silk. Modern modification also brought pockets, zippers, and other diverse changes to 한복. Nowadays, people usually wear 한복 only on special occasions such as weddings or traditional holidays.

USAGE

A   *Visiting a professor's office: How to start a conversation*

When you enter a professor's office, you can introduce yourself and state the reason for your visit as shown in the following dialogue:

마크:　　　　　저 . . . 여기가 김 교수님 연구실이지요?

김 교수님:　　네, 그런데요. 어떻게 오셨어요?

마크:　　　　　저는 마크 스미스입니다. 이번 학기에
　　　　　　　　한국어 수업을 듣고 싶습니다.

To ask the purpose of a visit, one says 어떻게 오셨어요? 'How can I help you?' (*lit.* How did you come?). Another way of asking is 무슨 일로 오셨어요? (*lit.* For what business did you come?).

 Exercise

Role-play: start a conversation in the following context:
A student visits a professor to take a placement test before taking a Korean class.

B   *Giving one's biographical information*

자기 소개 'self-introduction' may include the following information, among other things.

안녕하세요?

[이름]　　　　저는 마크 스미스입니다.

[고향]　　　　저는 호주 시드니에서 왔습니다.

　　　　　　　(or 제 고향은 ('hometown')

　　　　　　　호주 시드니예요.)

[학교]　　　　저는 서울대학교 대학원생입니다.

[전공]　　　　제 전공은 한국 역사입니다.

[집]　　　　　저는 학교 기숙사에서 삽니다.

[룸메이트]　　제 룸메이트는 한유진입니다.

Exercise 1

Introduce yourself.

Exercise 2

Interview a classmate and obtain the type of information given in the dialogue above. Then, introduce your classmate to the rest of the class based on what you have found out from the interview.

C   *Expressing reservations*

The connective form ~(으)ㄴ데/는데 is used to give background information for another situation. In conversation this pattern is also used to express reservations about someone or something, as illustrated below.

> A: 기숙사가 어때요?
>
> B: 학교에서 가까워서 좋은데 방이 좀 작아요.
>
> A: 룸메이트는 어때요?
>
> B: 착하고 좋은데 밤 늦게까지('until late at night') 음악을
>   자주 들어요.
>
> A: 기숙사 음식은 어때요?
>
> B: 다 괜찮은데 김치(*kimchi*)가 없어요.

Exercise

Make up dialogues on the following topics, using ~(으)ㄴ데/는데 whenever possible.

(1)   한국어 수업

(2)   요즘 날씨

(3)   (your school) 캠퍼스

(4)   학교 식당 음식

D Making an apology and giving reasons

When you apologize for being late for an appointment, use 늦어서 미안합니다 (or 늦어서 죄송합니다) 'I'm sorry for being late'. When you want to explain in detail your reason for being late, use the following pattern:

reason/cause: ~어서/아서 늦었습니다.

A: 오늘 왜 한국어 수업에 늦었어요?
B: a. 차가 많이 막혀서 늦었어요.
    Because traffic was congested.

   b. 차 사고가 나서 늦었어요.
    Because I had a car accident.

   c. 차가 고장이 나서 늦었어요.
    Because my car broke down.

   d. 늦잠을 자서 늦었어요.
    Because I overslept.

Exercise

Role-play: Using the question word '왜' and the clausal connective ~어서/아서, ask questions and provide reasons.

(1) A didn't come to school today and missed a test. A visits the professor to ask for a makeup.

(2) B was supposed to call A to set up a meeting time to do their assignment together, but B didn't.

(3) B invited A to his/her birthday party but A didn't show up.

Lesson 10 At a Professor's Office

CONVERSATION 1   *I don't have time today.*

Mark introduces himself to Professor Park and makes an arrangement to take the Korean placement test.

Mark: Hello, professor.

Professor: Yes, hello. How can I help you?

Mark: My name is Mark Smith. I'm majoring in Korean culture and I would like to take a Korean language class this semester.[G10.1–2]

Professor: Ah, really? How long have you been learning Korean?

Mark: I studied it for a year at Sydney University.[G10.3]

Professor: In that case, please take a Korean test this afternoon.

Mark: I'm sorry but I don't have time today.

Professor: Then come take it tomorrow morning at nine o'clock.

Mark: Yes sir, then I will see you tomorrow.

CONVERSATION 2   *I'm sorry for being late.*

Mark is late for the Korean placement test.

             (Knock knock)

Professor: Yes, come in.

Mark: I'm sorry for being late.[G10.4] There was a lot of traffic so I got delayed.

Professor: Seoul's traffic is pretty congested, isn't it? What did you take to get here?

Mark: There isn't a bus that comes directly here,[G10.5] so I took a taxi.

Professor: A taxi is also okay, but take the subway next time. The subway is fast and convenient.

Mark: What's the line number for the subway that comes here?

Professor: Line 2.

NARRATION	*Australian Student Mark*

I am Australian. I came to Seoul last month because I wanted to learn the Korean language and Korean culture. I studied Korean for one year in Australia. In Australia there are a lot of schools that teach Korean. This semester I am majoring in Korean culture at Seoul National University's graduate school. I am also taking a Korean class taught by Professor Park. Last month I took a Korean exam in Professor Park's office, but since there was a lot of traffic, I was 10 minutes late. In Seoul, the traffic is pretty congested and there are quite a lot of people. Traffic is inconvenient so I am moving into the school dormitories next week. However, there are a lot of interesting things too.

11과 기숙사 생활
Lesson 11 Living in a Dormitory

Conversation 1   차 한 잔 하실래요?

▌ Woojin and Minji meet at the school cafeteria.

Conversation   1

우진: 어, 민지 씨 아니세요? 뭐 하세요?

민지: 차 마시고 있어요.G11.1

　　　 우진 씨도 차 한 잔 하실래요?G11.2

우진: 네, 저도 마시고 싶었는데 잘 됐네요.

민지: 한국 생활이 어때요?

우진: 참 재미있어요. 친구도 많이 사귀었어요.

　　　 그리고 기숙사 생활도 편하고 재미있어요.

민지: 우진 씨는 방을 혼자 쓰세요?

우진: 아니요, 룸메이트가 있어요.

민지: 어떤 사람이에요?

우진: 호주에서 왔는데 한국 문화를 좋아하고

　　　 한국말도 잘 해요. 그리고 아주 친절하고 착해요.

NEW WORDS

NOUN

갈비	*galbi* (barbecued spareribs)
물	water
바닷가	beach
밴쿠버	Vancouver
불고기	*bulgogi* (roast meat)
생활	daily life, living
어젯밤	last night
차	② tea
청바지	blue jeans
캐나다	Canada

COUNTER

잔	glass, cup

PRE-NOUN

어떤	which, what kind of

VERB

되다	to become, get, turn into
눈(이) 오다	to snow
사귀다	to make friends
쓰다	② to use

ADJECTIVE

착하다	to be good-natured, kindhearted
친절하다	to be kind, considerate

SUFFIX

~(으)ㄹ래요	Would you like to . . . ?/ I would like to . . . (intention)
~고 있다	am/are/is ~ing

NEW EXPRESSIONS

1. 어, 민지 씨 아니세요? 'Oh, aren't you Minji?' expresses Woojin's surprise at meeting Minji unexpectedly.

2. 잘 됐네요 is an idiomatic expression, meaning 'It sounds good' (*lit.* It has turned out well). The dictionary form of 됐네요 is 되다 'to become, get, turn into'.

The verb 되다 has many functions, as shown below.

    a.   To become

        남동생은 내년에 대학생이 됩니다.   My younger brother will become a college student next year.

    b.   To work out, turn out

        참 잘 됐네요.   That's great (*lit.* It worked out well).

c.   Idiomatic expressions:

. . . 어떻게 됩니까/돼요?	What is/are . . . ?
주소가 어떻게 됩니까?	What is your address?
나이가 어떻게 되세요?	What is your age?
부모님 성함이 어떻게 되십니까?	What are your parents' names?

3. 사귀었어요 is often pronounced [사겨써요], although it is never written that way.

4. 어떤 is a noun-modifying form of 어떻다 'to be how' and denotes an unspecified person or thing. 어떤 occurs both as an interrogative meaning 'what kind (type) of?' and as an indefinite, 'certain, some'.

Exercises

1. Connect each of the phrases from the left column with a predicate on the right.

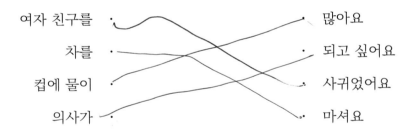

여자 친구를	많아요
차를	되고 싶어요
컵에 물이	사귀었어요
의사가	마셔요

2. Answer the following questions:

(1)   어떤 일을 하고 싶어요?

(2)   어떤 친구를 사귀고 싶어요?

(3)   어떤 음악을 듣고 싶어요?

(4)   어떤 생일 선물을 받고 싶어요?

Grammar

G11.1   The progressive form ~고 있다

(1) 남동생은 친구하고 불고기를 만들**고 있어요**.

(2) A: 지금 뭐 하**고 있어요**?   What are you doing now?

B: 음악 듣**고 있어요**.   I'm listening to music.

(3) 지금 밖에 눈이 오**고 있어요**.

(4) 아버지는 신문을 읽**고 계세요**.   My father is reading the newspaper.

Examples

Notes

1. ~고 있다 expresses the continuation or progression of an action. Only verbs (not adjectives) can occur in this construction.

2. Various forms of ~고 있다:

	Default forms	Plain	Subject honorific
Non-past	~고 있다	~고 있어요	~고 계세요
Past	~고 있었다	~고 있었어요	~고 계셨어요

동생은 방에서 놀고 있어요

저는 어젯밤 9시에 친구하고 전화하고 있었어요.

어머니는 지금 영화를 보고 계세요.

아침에 아버지는 신문을 보고 계셨어요.

Exercises

1. Change the verbs into the progressive form ~고 있다 or ~고 계시다.

    (1) 동생이 방에서 (자다)   <u>자고 있어요</u>.

    (2) 저는 지금 도서관에서 (일하다)   _____

    (3) 부모님께서 캐나다 밴쿠버에서 (살다)   _____

    (4) 소피아는 교실에서 (공부하다)   _____

    (5) 마크는 마이클하고 책을 같이 (쓰다)   _____

2. Practice with your partner as in the example.

    (1)   A: 동수는 지금 뭐 하고 있어요?

                    B: 자전거를 타고 있어요.

    (2) 수미   (3) 유미   (4) 마이클   (5) 제니

3. Practice the above dialogues one more time using the past-tense form ~고 있었어요 as in the example.

    A: 동수는 어제 아침에 뭐 하고 있었어요?

    B: 자전거를 타고 있었어요.

4. Describe each person's activity, using the construction [~고 있는] + N (see G10.5), and ask your partner who each one of them is.

(1)   A: 자전거를 타고 있는 사람은 누구예요?
                            B: 동수예요.

(2) 린다   (3) 수잔   (4) 마이클   (5) 팀

(6) 스티브   (7) 수미   (8) 폴   (9) 마이클 & 유미

G11.2   Intentional ~(으)ㄹ래요

(1) A: 뭐 **먹을래요?**   What would you like to eat?
     B: 저는 갈비 **먹을래요.**   I'd like to eat *galbi.*
     C: 저는 불고기 **먹을래요.**   I'd like to eat *bulgogi.*

(2) A: 이번 주말에 영화 보러 **갈래요?**
     B: 네, 좋아요. 같이 가요.

(3) A: 물 좀 **주실래요?**   Would you give me some
                                        water?

     B: 네, 여기 있어요.

Notes

1. ~(으)ㄹ래요 is used to ask the intention of the listener in questions and refers to the speaker's intention in statements.

2. ~(으)ㄹ래요? in questions is used in less formal settings. A more formal and polite form is ~(으)시겠어요?

3. The formation of ~(으)ㄹ래요 with verbs in /ㄷ/ and /ㄹ/ is demonstrated below.

Dictionary form	~어요/아요	~(으)ㄹ래요
걷다 to walk	걸어요	걸을래요
만들다 to make	만들어요	만들래요

Exercises

1. Change the verbs in the box below with different suffixes.

	오다	먹다	타다	듣다
~어요/아요			타요	
~(으)ㄹ래요	올래요			
~(스)ㅂ니다		먹습니다		

2. Practice as in the example.

(1) 뭐 마실 거예요?   (커피)   <u>커피 마실래요.</u>

(2) 무슨 영화 볼 거예요?   (액션 영화)   _____

(3) 무슨 옷을 살 거예요?   (청바지)   _____

(4) 주말에 어디 갈 거예요?   (바닷가)   _____

(5) 뭐 먹을 거예요?   (불고기)   _____

(6) 내일 저녁에 뭐 할 거예요?   _____

CULTURE

한국의 음악 (Music in Korea)

At the center of 한류, the worldwide surge of popularity of Korean pop culture, are Korean popular songs. Widely known as K-pop, Korean popular songs have generated interest in Korea and its culture all around the world. However, even before the rise of popular K-pop groups such as 방탄소년단 (BTS) and singers such as 싸이 (PSY), there were Korean artists who directed the attention of the world to the musical talent of Koreans. 장영주 (Sarah Chang), a Korean-American violin prodigy, surprised the world with her musical talent from the age of eight. 장한나 (Han-Na Chang) is a world-class cellist who won the Rostropovich Cello Competition at the age of 11 and, after which, began studying under the famous cello maestro Rostropovich. 조수미 (Sumi Jo) captivated the hearts of the world with her heavenly soprano voice, while 정명훈 (Myung-Whun Chung) enjoyed a splendid career as an orchestra conductor in the field of Western classical music. 조성진 (Seong-Jin Cho) was the first Korean pianist to be awarded First Prize at the Chopin International Piano Competition, and continues to receive much attention and love around the world.

In the field of traditional Korean music, 김덕수 (Duk-Soo Kim) left an outstanding legacy. He modified traditional 풍물놀이 into 사물놀이. As opposed to the larger-scale, activity-oriented 풍물놀이, his new breed of traditional Korean music incorporated the sophisticated qualities of quartet performances. The advent of 사물놀이 triggered the introduction of traditional Korean music to the world and helped to inspire many musicians to venture into this new area of traditional Korean music.

| Conversation 2 | 연극 보러 갈까요? |

Minji and Woojin chat in the dormitory lounge.

Conversation   2

우진: 시간이 참 빠르지요? 벌써 한 학기가 다
       끝났어요. 이번 학기에 몇 과목 들었어요?

민지: 다섯 과목 들었어요.

우진: 다섯 과목이나^{G11.3} 들었어요?
       저는 세 과목밖에^{G11.3} 안 들었어요.

민지: 월요일부터 금요일까지 매일 수업이 있어서
       너무 바빴어요. 우진 씨는 이번 학기 잘 보냈어요?

우진: 숙제가 많아서 저도 좀 바빴어요.
       다음 주부터는 좀 쉬고 싶어요.

민지: 그럼 시험 끝나고 같이 연극 보러 갈까요?^{G11.4}

우진: 네, 좋아요.

민지: 보고 싶은 연극 있어요?

우진: 글쎄요.

민지: 인터넷으로 같이 알아볼까요?

우진: 네, 그래요.

NEW WORDS

NOUN

골프	golf
기차	train
연극	play
인터넷	internet
입구	entrance

VERB

끝나다	to be over, finished
쉬다	to rest
알아보다	to find out, check out
찾다	to find, look for
춤(을) 추다	to dance

ADJECTIVE

| 힘(이) 들다 | to be hard, difficult |

ADVERB

| 다 | all |
| 벌써 | already |

PARTICLE

까지	② to/until/through (time)
밖에	nothing but, only
부터	from (time) . . .
(이)나	as much/many as

SUFFIX

| ~(으)ㄹ까요? | Shall I/we . . . ?; Do you think that . . . ? |
| 글쎄요 | Well; It's hard to say |

NEW EXPRESSIONS

1. The pattern [time]부터 [time]까지 'from . . . to . . .' is usually used for temporal expressions. [Place]에서 [place]까지, though also translated 'from . . . to . . .', is used for location (Lesson 6, Conversation 1).

부터: a starting point in time or location 'from'

까지: an ending point in time or location '(all the way) to, until, through'

Time: . . . 부터 . . . 까지
한국어 수업은 9시부터 10시까지 있어요.
아침부터 저녁까지 일해요.

Location: . . . 에서 . . . 까지
서울에서 뉴욕까지 비행기로 얼마나 걸려요?
기숙사에서 교실까지 걸어서 얼마나 걸려요?

2. 글쎄요 'Well (I am not quite sure)' is used when one is not quite ready to give an answer. It can also be used to show hesitation or to express a refusal in a polite and indirect way.

A: 이번 주에 같이 영화 보러 갈래요?

B: 글쎄요. 다음 주에 시험이 있는데요.

Exercise

Answer the following questions using 부터and 까지.

(1) 몇 시부터 몇 시까지 자요?

(2) 오늘 수업이 언제 있어요?

(3) 언제부터 한국어를 배웠어요?

(4) 언제부터 [뉴욕, 보스턴, 로스앤젤레스, . . .]에서 살았어요?

(5) 한국어 수업은 몇 시부터 몇 시까지 있어요?

Notes

Grammar

G11.3   N(이)나 vs. N밖에

(1)   A: 이번 학기에 몇 과목 들었어요?   How many classes did you take this semester?

B: 다섯 과목 들었어요.   I took five classes.

A: 다섯 과목**이나** 들었어요?   You took five [that many]?

저는 세 과목**밖에** 안 들었는데요.   I took only three.

(2)   A: 집에서 학교까지 얼마나 걸려요?   How long does it take from your home to school?

B: 걸어서 5분**밖에** 안 걸려요.   It takes only five minutes on foot.

A: 아, 그래요?
저는 차로 한 시간**이나** 걸려요.

(3) 남자 시계를 찾는데 여자 시계**밖에** 없어요.

Notes

1. When attached to an expression of quantity, the particle (이)나 indicates that the quantity in question is more than the speaker's expectation. It shows surprise or shock at the large quantity. (이)나 can often be translated 'as much/many as', but it also implies 'that many/much' along with an expression of quantity, as in (1). 이나 is used when the expression ends in a consonant, 나 when the expression ends in a vowel.

파티에 스무 명이나 왔어요. vs. 내일 시험이 다섯 개나 있어요.

2. [N밖에 + negative] 'nothing/nobody/no . . . but N; only N' is used when the speaker feels that the amount of the item mentioned is smaller than the speaker's expectation. Compare the answers in (a) and (b) below.

A: 교실에서 기숙사 입구까지 얼마나 걸려요?

B: (a) 걸어서 5분 걸려요.   It takes five minutes on foot.

(neutral description)

(b) 걸어서 5분밖에 안 걸려요.   It takes only five minutes on foot.

(less than expected)

More examples are given below.

A: 파티에 누가 왔어요?

B: 마크밖에 안 왔어요.

A: 어제 몇 시간 잤어요?

B: 세 시간밖에 못 잤어요.

3. [N밖에 + negative] is not used in commands; 만 'only' is used instead.

한국어로만 말하세요.

경제학 숙제만 하세요.

Exercises

1. Using (이)나 or 밖에, indicate your surprise at the quantity.

(1) A: 파티에 사람들 많이 왔어요?

B: 네, 여덟 명 왔어요.

A: <u>여덟 명 밖에 안 왔어요?</u>

(2) A: 이번 학기에 몇 과목 들으세요?

B: 여섯 과목 들어요.

A: <u>여섯 과목에를 들어요?</u>

(3)　A:　어제 잘 잤어요?

　　　B:　4시간쯤 잤어요.

　　　A:　*4시간쯤 밖에 안 잤어요*

(4)　A:　한국어 숙제 했어요?

　　　B:　네, 그런데 _____

　　　A:　저도 5시간 걸렸어요.

(5)　A:　스타워즈 (*Star Wars*) 영화 봤어요?

　　　B:　네, 너무 재미있어서 *10번이나 봤어요*

　　　A:　그래요? 저도 세 번 봤어요.

2. Answer the following questions, using (이)나 or 밖에.

(1)　A:　어제 많이 잤어요?　　　　　　[7시간]

　　　B:　a. 일곱 시간밖에 못 잤어요.

　　　　　b. 일곱 시간이나 잤어요.

(2)　돈이 얼마 있어요?　　　　　　　　[100불]

(3)　집에 책이 많이 있어요?　　　　　　[40권]

(4)　교실에 의자가 몇 개 있어요?　　　　[6개]

(5)　지난 주에 시험 있었어요?　　　　　[4개]

(6)　한국어 수업에 학생이 많아요?　　　[20명]

(7)　어제 파티에 사람들이 많이 왔어요?　[12명]

G11.4   Asking someone's opinion: ~(으)ㄹ까요?

Examples

(1) 한국어로 말**할까요**?   Shall I/we speak in Korean?

(2) 내일 날씨가 좋**을까요**?   Do you think tomorrow's
                                            weather will be good?

(3) 기차로 갈까요, 버스로 **갈까요**?   Shall I/we go by train or by
                                            bus?

(4) 일이 **힘들까요**?   Do you think the work will
                                            be hard?

Notes

1. The basic function of ~(으)ㄹ까요? is to ask for the listener's opinion. When the speaker is (a part of) the subject, ~(으)ㄹ까요 often connotes a suggestion or an offer ("shall I/we?") in addition to asking the listener's opinion. This structure is strictly a question. It cannot be used to mean "I shall do."

뭘 먹을까요?	What shall we eat?
갈비 먹을까요?	Shall we eat *galbi*? / How about eating *galbi*?
커피 마실까요?	Shall we drink some coffee?
제가 갈까요?	Shall I go? (= May I suggest that I go?)

2. When the subject is a third person, ~(으)ㄹ까요? 'Do you think that . . . ?' is used to seek the listener's opinion.

시험이 어려울까요?	Do you think that the exam will be difficult?
제니가 파티에 올까요?	Do you think that Jenny will come to the party?

3. The pattern ~(으)ㄹ까요? is also used for questions that offer a choice of alternatives, as in 영어로 말할까요, 한국어로 말할까요? 'Shall I/we speak in English or shall I/we speak in Korean?' Notice that in Korean the whole predicate is repeated, whereas in English the predicate is not repeated often (e.g., Shall I/we speak in English or in Korean?).

4. The form ~(으)ㄹ까요? has the following variations:

   a. ~을까요? occurs after a verb or adjective stem ending in a consonant other than /ㄹ/.

   b. ~ㄹ까요? occurs after a verb or adjective stem ending in a vowel.

   c. ~까요? occurs after a verb or adjective stem ending in /ㄹ/.

	Dictionary form		~(으)ㄹ까요?
Stems ending in a consonant	먹다	to eat	먹을까요
	앉다	to sit down	앉을까요
	좋다	to be good	좋을까요
Stems ending in a vowel	만나다	to meet	만날까요
	말하다	to speak	말할까요
	크다	to be big	클까요
Stems with /ㄹ/	살다	to live	살까요
	멀다	to be far	멀까요
Stems with /ㅂ/	가깝다	to be near	가까울까요

When irregular predicates in /ㅂ/ occur with the ~(으)ㄹ까요? form, /ㅂ/ is changed to 우, as shown below.

가깝다	to be near	가까울까요
어렵다	to be difficult	어려울까요
쉽다	to be easy	쉬울까요

(Exceptions: 좁다 → 좁을까요, 넓다 → 넓을까요)

Exercises

1. Translate the following sentences into Korean.

(1) Shall I call Lisa?

_____

(2) Shall we play tennis together this weekend?

_____

(3) What time shall I come tomorrow morning?

_____

(4) Will the test be easy or difficult?

_____

(5) Do you think that Sophia will come to the party?

_____

2. Make alternative sentences using ~(으)ㄹ까요? as in the example.

(1) 한국어 / 영어, 말하다
   A:　　한국어로 말할까요, 영어로 말할까요?
   B:　　한국어로 말하세요.

(2) 택시 / 버스, 타다
   A:　_____
   B:　_____

(3) 커피 / 차, 마시다
   A:　_____
   B:　_____

(4) 한국어 / 일본어, 연습하다
   A:　_____
   B:　_____

(5) 테니스 / 골프, 치다
   A:　_____
   B:　_____

Narration 　　　캐나다 학생 민지

저는 서울에서 한국어를 배우고 있는 캐나다 학생입니다. 밴쿠버에서 왔고 나이는 스물두 살입니다. 지금 학교 기숙사에서 삽니다. 지난 학기 동안 저는 기숙사에서 여러 친구들을 사귀었습니다. 3층에 사는 우진 씨는 미국에서 왔습니다. 우진 씨는 운동도 잘하고, 공부도 열심히 하고, 아주 친절합니다. 우진 씨는 호주 학생인 마크하고 방을 같이 씁니다. 마크 씨도 아주 친절하고 착한 친구입니다. 저는 우진 씨하고 마크 씨하고 기숙사 식당에서 자주 저녁을 먹습니다. 다음 주에 시험이 모두 끝납니다. 그래서 시험 끝나고 같이 연극을 보러 갈 겁니다.

Exercise

Read the narration and answer the following questions.

(1) 민지는 한국에서 무엇을 하고 있습니까?

(2) 우진이는 어디에서 왔고, 어떤 학생입니까?

(3) 우진의 룸메이트는 누구입니까?

(4) 민지는 누구하고 자주 저녁을 먹습니까?

(5) 다음 주에는 무슨 일이 있습니까?

USAGE

A   *Meeting someone by chance*

When you run into someone you know, you can greet the person by saying
any of the following:

민정 씨 아니세요?	Isn't this Minjung?
선생님, 안녕하세요?	Hello, professor.
스티브 씨, 뭐 하세요?	Hi, Steve. What you are doing?
오래간만이에요.	Long time no see.
반가워요.	(I'm) happy to see you.
어디 가세요?	Where are you going? (You do not necessarily expect an answer to this question.)
여기 웬 일이세요?	What brought you here?

Exercise

Suppose you came across the following people in the following places. How
would you start a conversation? Make up a dialogue, using the models shown
above.

(1)   Meet a teacher on campus.
(2)   Meet a classmate in front of the dormitory elevator.
(3)   Meet a friend on the street whom you haven't seen for a long time.
(4)   Meet an acquaintance at the post office.

B   *Extending, accepting, and declining invitations*

When you are inviting someone over or asking about going out with someone, you normally start out by asking if the person has time.

A: 이번 주말에 시간 있어요?

B: 네, 괜찮아요.

A: 그럼, 춤추러 클럽('club')에 갈래요?

B: 네, 좋아요. 같이 가요.

Exercise 1

Adapt the preceding dialogue to the pictures below.

(1)   (2)   (3)

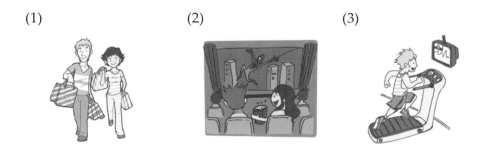

When you are accepting an invitation, simply say 네. In declining an invitation, the sentence ending ~(으)ㄴ데요/는데요 is often used to soften the refusal (see G10.3).

A: 이번 주말에 영화 보러 갈래요?

B: 글쎄요. 좀 바쁜데요.

A: 그럼 다음 주말에는 어때요?

B: 미안해요. 다음 주말에는 벌써 약속이 있는데요.

The following pattern is commonly used when making suggestions.

[Purpose](으)러 [place]에 _____~(으)ㄹ래요?

Exercise 2

Practice the following dialogue based on the pictures.

(1)

A: 스티브 씨, 안녕하세요?

B: 유미 씨, 오래간만이에요.

         어디 가세요?

A: 책 사러 서점에 가요.

B: 어, 저도 책 사러 서점에 가는데요.

A: 그럼, 같이 갈래요?

B: 네, 같이 가요.

(2)

(3)

(4)

(5)

C   *Setting up a get-together*

Exercise

민지: 우진 씨, 오늘 날씨도 좋은데 테니스 같이 안 칠래요?

우진: 그래요. 그럼 오늘 칠까요?

민지: 몇 시에 시간 있으세요?

우진: 점심 먹고 2시 30분쯤 어때요?

민지: 좋아요. 어디서 만날까요?

우진: 1층 라운지('lounge')에서 만날까요?

Key grammatical patterns to use:

~(으)ㄴ데/는데   to explain the backgroud for the get-together

~(으)ㄹ래요?   to ask the other person's intention for the meeting

~(으)ㄹ까요?   to ask the other person's opinion of your choice

                                    (of time and place)

Exercise 1

Break into groups to organize the following activities. Report the arrangements you've made to the class.

    (1)   주말 운동
    (2)   친구 생일 파티
    (3)   주말 여행
    (4)   크리스마스 파티

Exercise 2

Call the following places and set up appointments or reservations for the reasons specified.

    (1)   이태리 식당: 가족들과 같이 맛있는 저녁을
                                     먹고 싶어서

    (2)   교수님 연구실: 모르는 것이 많아서

    (3)   컴퓨터 랩: 한국어 시험이 있어서
                                     연습하고 싶어서

Lesson 11 Living in a Dormitory

CONVERSATION 1   *Would you like a cup of tea?*

Woojin and Minji meet at the school cafeteria.

Woojin: Oh, aren't you Minji? What are you up to?

Minji: I'm drinking tea.[G11.1] Would you like a cup of tea too, Woojin?[G11.2]

Woojin: Yes, I wanted to drink some too, so this works out.

Minji: How do you like living in Korea?

Woojin: It's really fun. I made a lot of friends, and living in the dormitory is convenient and fun.

Minji: Do you have your own room, Woojin?

Woojin: No, I have a roommate.

Minji: What kind of person are they?

Woojin: He's from Australia, likes Korean culture, and also speaks Korean well. He's very friendly and nice too.

CONVERSATION 2   *Shall we go see a play?*

Minji and Woojin chat in the dormitory lounge.

Woojin: Time sure goes by quickly doesn't it? One semester has already finished. How many courses did you take this semester?

Minji: I took five courses.

Woojin: You took as many as five courses?[G11.3] I took only three courses.[G11.3]

Minji: I had classes every day from Monday to Friday, so I was very busy. Did you have a good semester, Woojin?

Woojin: There was a lot of homework, so I was a little busy too. Starting from next week, I'd like to rest for a little bit.

Minji: Then shall we go see a play together after exams are finished?[G11.4]

Woojin: Yeah, great!

Minji: Is there a play you'd like to see?

Woojin: Well . . .

Minji: Shall we look into it together online?

Woojin: Yeah, let's do that!

NARRATION   *Canadian student Minji*

I am a Canadian student learning Korean in Seoul. I am from Vancouver and am twenty-two years old. I live in the school dormitory now. Last semester, I made several friends in the dormitories. Woojin, who lives on the 3rd floor, came from the United States. Woojin is athletic, studies hard, and is very friendly. Woojin shares a room with Mark, who is an Australian student. Mark is also a very kind and nice friend. I often eat dinner with Woojin and Mark at the dormitory cafeteria. All exams will be over next week, so we plan to go see a play together.

12과 가족

Lesson 12 Family

Conversation 1   어디서 오셨어요?

▍Students introduce themselves in a classroom.

Conversation 1

마크:	민지 씨, 어디서 오셨어요?
민지:	캐나다 밴쿠버에서 왔어요. 거기서 태어나서G12.1 자랐어요.
마크:	가족들이 다 밴쿠버에 사세요?
민지:	아니요, 부모님만 거기 계시고, 형제들은 다 다른 데에 살아요.
마크:	형제가 많으세요?
민지:	네, 저까지 넷이에요. 저는 둘째예요. 오빠 한 명하고 동생 두 명이 있어요. 마크 씨 가족은 어디 사세요?
마크:	부모님은 시드니에 계시고, 형은 결혼해서 미국 동부에서 살아요. 막내는 영국에서 공부하고 있는데 다음 주에 서울에 와요.
민지:	아, 그래요? 좋겠어요.G12.2

NEW WORDS

NOUN

데	place
동부	East Coast
막내	youngest child
바지	pants
밤	night
부엌	kitchen
셔츠	shirt
형제	sibling(s)

PRE-NOUN

첫	first

ADJECTIVE

다르다	to be different
피곤하다	to be tired

VERB

결혼하다	to get married
기다리다	to wait
자라다	to grow up
태어나다	to be born

ADVERB

아직	still, yet

PARTICLE

까지	③ including

COUNTER

째/번째	ordinal numbers

SUFFIX

~겠	may, will (conjecture)
~어서/아서	② clausal connective (sequential)

NEW EXPRESSIONS

1. 형제 is the contracted form of 형제자매 'brothers and sisters', meaning siblings.

2. For ordinal numbers (e.g., first, second, third), native numbers (except for 첫 'first') are used with the ordinal counters 번째 as in 첫 (번째) 비행기 'first flight', 두 번째 수업 'second class', 세 번째 시험 'third exam'. The ordinal counter 째 is usually used with some kinship terms such as 첫(째) 아들 'first son', 둘째 딸 'second daughter', 셋째 언니 'third older sister'.

첫(째)	첫 번째	first
둘째	두 번째	second
셋째	세 번째	third
넷째	네 번째	fourth
다섯째	다섯 번째	fifth
열째	열 번째	tenth
스무째	스무 번째	twentieth

Exercises

1. Fill in the blanks with your information.

저는 _____에서 태어났어요. 그리고 _____에서

자랐어요. _____에서 고등학교를 졸업('graduation')했어요.

대학교를 졸업하고 _____에서 일하고 싶어요. 그리고

결혼해서 _____에서 살고 싶어요.

2. Find out who has the most and fewest siblings among your classmates.
Also find out whether they are the first, middle, or last child.

A: 형제가 몇 명이에요 / 어떻게 되세요?

B: 저까지 _____ 명이에요.

A: 몇 째예요?

B: [첫째, 둘째, 셋째, 막내 . . .]예요.

Grammar

G12.1   The clausal connective ~어서/아서 (sequential)

(1)   서점에 **가서**   I went to the bookstore, then
       사전하고 지도를 샀어요.   bought a dictionary and a map.

(2)   아침에 **일어나서** 운동했어요.   I got up in the morning, then
                                          exercised.

(3)   친구를 **만나서** 저녁 먹고   I met my friend; then we had dinner
       같이 영화 보러 갔어요.   and went to see a movie together.

Examples

Notes

1. The suffix ~어서/아서 connects two clauses. It has two main functions: (a) to provide a cause-and-effect relationship between two events (G10.4) and (b) to state actions or events in chronological sequence.

   a. The function of ~어서/아서 'and so' in indicating a cause-and-effect relationship between events.

   b. ~어서/아서 '(and) then' can be used to link two sequential, tightly related events that do not have a cause-and-effect relationship, as shown in the examples.

2. ~어서/아서 clauses cannot have a past-tense form of the verb. The subjects of the clauses connected by the sequential ~어서/아서 must be the same, whereas for the causal ~어서/아서, the subjects can be different.

집에 가**서** 잤어요.	(I) went home and (then) slept. (sequential)
날씨가 좋**아서** 바닷가에 놀러 갔어요.	The weather was good, (and) so (we) went to the beach to play. (causal)

3. Compare ~어서/아서 with ~고. Both forms indicate a sequence of events. However, they differ in the following ways:

~어서/아서 connects two sequential events, with the second event always a result of the first. Even when the first event does not cause the second, it is a precondition for the second event. In contrast, the basic meaning of ~고 is simply to list two or more events, and there is no implication that the first event leads to the second.

   a. 친구를 만나서 영화를 보러 갔어요. I met my friend, and (then) we went to see a movie.

   b. 친구를 만나고 영화를 보러 갔어요. I met my friend, and I went to see a movie.

In (a), when ~어서/아서 is used, it means that the speaker went to the movie with the friend. In (b), the speaker met the friend and then went to see a movie (with someone else or alone). Thus, ~고 simply lists two events without implying that they are related. Consider another pair of examples:

> c. 백화점에 가서 선물을 샀어요.   I went to a department store and (then) bought a present (there).
>
> d. 백화점에 가고 선물을 샀어요.   I went to a department store; I (also) bought a present (somewhere else).

In (c), the speaker went to a department store and bought a present there and nowhere else. In (d), when 고 is used, there is no implication that the speaker bought a present at that particular department store.

Exercises

1. Combine the two sequential events using the ~어서/아서 form, as shown in the example.

    (1) 아침 6시에 일어났어요. 운동했어요.

          <u>아침 6시에 일어나서 운동했어요.</u>

    (2) 오후에 친구를 만났어요. 같이 영화 보러 갔어요.

          _____

    (3) 어제 옷가게에 갔어요. 셔츠하고 바지를 샀어요.

          _____

    (4) 의자에 앉으세요. 기다리세요.

          _____

    (5) 부모님께 편지를 썼어요. 부모님께 보냈어요.

          _____

2. Answer the question 어제 뭐 했어요? using [place]에 가서 ~었/았어요.

(1) A: 어제 뭐 했어요?
    B: 도서관에 가서 공부했어요.

(2)

(3)

(4)

(5)

Grammar

G12.2   Conjectural ~겠~

(1) A: 내일 뉴욕에서 오빠가 와요.

B: 아, 그래요?   Is that right?

좋**겠**어요.   (I guess that) you must be
                             excited.

(2) A: 어제 시험이 세 개나 있었어요.

B: 힘들**었겠**어요.

(3) A: 알**겠**어요?   Do you understand?

B: a. 모르**겠**어요.   (I'm afraid that) I don't
                             understand.

b. 네, 알**겠**어요.   (I guess) I understand.

Notes

1. ~겠~ can be used to express the speaker's guess or conjecture (and to ask the listener's guess or conjecture in questions) based on the circumstantial evidence or given information. It can be glossed in English as "I guess/think . . ." and "You must be . . ."

A: 점심 먹었어요?

B: 아니요, 시간이 없어서 아직 못 먹었어요.

A: 벌써 3시인데, 배 고프('be hungry')겠어요.

2. In making a conjecture about a past or completed event, ~었/았겠어요 is used as shown in example (2).

3. In its extended function, the conjectural suffix ~겠~ can be used to raise the level of politeness. As in example (3), 알겠어요 and 모르겠어요 sound more polite than 알아요 and 몰라요.

Exercise

Comment on the following situations, using the ~겠어요 form.

(1) A: 어머니께서 부엌에서 갈비를 만들고 계세요.

    B: (맛있다) <u>맛있겠어요</u>.

(2) A: 텔레비전을 너무 많이 봤어요.

    B: (머리가 아프다) _____

(3) A: 어제 밤에 세 시간밖에 못 잤어요.

    B: (피곤하다) _____

(4) A: 내일 여동생이 영국에서 첫 비행기로 와요.

    B: (좋다) _____

(5) A: 교통이 무척 복잡해요.

    B: (학교에 늦다) _____

Notes

· ·

· ·

· ·

· ·

· ·

· ·

Conversation 2   가족 사진이 잘 나왔네요.

Minji and Woojin talk about their families.

Conversation   2

민지: 부모님 연세가 어떻게 되세요?

우진: 아버지는 쉰다섯이시고 어머니는 쉰셋이세요.

여기 우리 가족 사진이 있는데 보실래요?

민지: 어머, 사진이 참 잘 나왔네요.G12.3

이 사진 언제 찍었어요?

우진: 작년 할머니 생신에 찍었어요.

민지: 여기 노란G12.4 한복을 입은G12.5 분이 할머니세요?

우진: 네.

민지: 여기 키가 큰 분이 형님이시지요?

우진: 네, 우리 형이에요. 지금 대학원에 다녀요.

민지: 우진 씨가 형님이랑 눈이 닮았네요.

NEW WORDS

NOUN

눈	① eyes; ② snow
색	color (=색깔)
안경	eyeglasses
한복	traditional Korean dress
형님 *hon.*	male's older brother

VERB

끼다	to wear (glasses, gloves, rings)
나오다	to come out
다니다	to attend
닮다	to resemble
쓰다	③ to wear headgear
입다	to wear, put on (clothes)

PARTICLE

(이)랑	with, and

ADJECTIVE

까맣다	to be black
노랗다 (노란)	to be yellow
빨갛다	to be red
키가 작다	to be short (height)
키가 크다	to be tall (height)
파랗다	to be blue
하얗다	to be white

ADVERB

또	② also, too
오래	long time

INTERJECTION

어머	Oh my! Dear me!

SUFFIX

~네요	sentence ending indicating the speaker's reaction
~(으)ㄴ	noun-modifying form (past)

NEW EXPRESSIONS

1. In 우진 씨가 형님이랑 눈이 닮았어요 '(His eyes) resemble yours, Woojin', 닮았어요 is in the past-tense form but actually denotes a present state. N(이)랑 닮았다 is a pattern meaning 'to resemble N', as in 저는 엄마랑 닮았어요.

2. Colors (색/색깔):

Dictionary form	Color	Color noun
노랗다	yellow	노랑/노란색
하얗다	white	하양/하얀색
까맣다	black	까망/까만색
빨갛다	red	빨강/빨간색
파랗다	blue	파랑/파란색

More colors:

초록색	**green**	**보라색**	**purple**
주황색	orange	밤색/갈색	brown
분홍색	pink	회색	gray

3. Clothing:

Korean has different verbs for 'to put on, wear', depending on how the item is worn.

	Item	to put on, wear	to take off
옷 셔츠 치마 바지	clothes shirts skirts pants/trousers	입다 (apparel other than headgear, footwear, gloves)	벗다
모자	hats, caps	쓰다 (headgear)	벗다
안경	eyeglasses	쓰다/끼다	벗다
신(발) 운동화 양말	footwear sneakers socks/stockings	신다 (footwear)	벗다
장갑 반지	gloves rings	끼다 (things that fit tightly)	벗다 (gloves) 빼다 (rings)
목걸이 귀걸이	necklaces earrings	하다	빼다
시계	wristwatches	차다	풀다
벨트 넥타이	belts ties	하다/매다	풀다
가방	backpacks/purses	메다/들다	

Note that the verb 하다 can be used with necklaces, earrings, and other accessories except 시계.

Exercises

1. Fill in the blanks with the color terms.

    (1) 머리: <u>까만색</u>

    (2) 눈: _____

    (3) 바지: _____

    (4) 가방: _____

    (5) 좋아하는 색깔: _____

    (6) 자주 입는 옷 색깔: _____

2. Connect the corresponding nouns and predicates.

        사진을 ·   · 다녀요.

         옷을 ·   · 닮았어요.

        형제가 ·   · 찍어요.

      대학원에 ·   · 와요.

         눈이 ·   · 입어요.

3. Fill in the blanks with your information.

    (1) 저는 _____(이)랑 눈이 닮았어요.

    (2) 저는 _____(이)랑 얼굴('face')이 닮았어요.

    (3) 저는 _____(이)랑 성격('personality')이 닮았어요.

    (4) 저는 아버지/어머니랑 _____이/가 닮았어요.

4. Fill in the blanks with the appropriate clothing/accessory items.

    (1) _____을/를 입어요

    (2) _____을/를 신어요.

    (3) _____을/를 써요

    (4) _____을/를 해요.

5. Describe what you are wearing.

> **Example**
>
> 저는 하얀 셔츠하고 파란 바지를 입고
> 안경을 썼어요.

6. Find out the following information.

   (1)   오늘 청바지를 입은 사람이 누구예요?

   (2)   오늘 모자를 쓴 사람이 있어요? 무슨 색 모자를 썼어요?

   (3)   교실에 안경을 낀 사람이 몇 명 있어요?

   (4)   학생들이 좋아하는 셔츠 색이 뭐예요?

Grammar

G12.3   The sentence ending ~네요

Examples

(1)   저기 스티브가 **오네요**.   Steve is coming there.

(2)   A: 미국에서 얼마나 살았어요?   How long have you lived in the United States?

        B: 15년 살았어요.   I have lived (in the United States) for fifteen years.

        A: 미국에서 오래 **살았네요**.   You have lived in the United States for a long time.

(3)   A: 어제 밤 2시까지 공부했어요.   I studied until 2 a.m. last night.

        B: 피곤**하겠네요**.   You must be tired.

Notes

1. The sentence ending ~네요 expresses the speaker's spontaneous reaction (such as surprise, admiration, or sympathy) to some new information.

2. Compare ~네요 with ~어요/아요. ~어요/아요 is simply informative; ~네요 also carries the speaker's emotion, which is frequently contrary to what the speaker had been expecting. For example, compare the two sentences below:

> a. 소피아가 벌써 학교에 갔어요. Sophia already went to school.
>
> b. 소피아가 벌써 학교에 갔**네요**. (To my surprise) Sophia already went to school.

The speaker in (b) was thinking that Sophia had not gone to school yet, but finds that she has. Thus, ~네요 is used when expectations conflict with facts, causing surprise (or some other feeling).

3. The conjecture suffix ~겠 and the ending ~네요 can be combined to express the speaker's realization of what would happen to the given input. In (3), the meaning of 피곤하겠네요 is '[I guess] you must be tired!' and speaker B says this in reaction to what speaker A said about himself.

Exercise

Change the following sentence endings into the ~네요 form, as in the example.

(1) 오늘 날씨가 아주 더워요.   오늘 날씨가 아주 덥네요.

(2) 옷이 참 예뻐요.   _____

(3) 제 안경이 여기 있어요.   _____

(4) 마크가 아직 집에 안 왔어요.   _____

(5) 시험이 어려워요.   _____

(6) 바지가 너무 커요.   _____

(7) 제니는 키가 작아요.   _____

G12.4   Irregular predicates with /ㅎ/

(1)   저는 **노란** 색을 좋아해요.   I like the color yellow.

(2)   **이런** 모자는 **어때요**?   How about this kind of hat?

(3)   제 머리는 **까매요**.   My hair is black.

Notes

1. Some adjective stems ending in the consonant /ㅎ/ drop the stem-final /ㅎ/ before a vowel. This irregular pattern applies mostly to color terms and demonstrative adjectives such as 이렇다/그렇다/저렇다 'to be this/that way'. The irregular pattern is illustrated below with 노랗다 'to be yellow'.

노랗 + ~은	→	노란
노랗 + ~아요	→	노래요
노랗 + ~아서	→	노래서
노랗 + ~을까요?	→	노랄까요?
노랗 + ~았어요	→	노랬어요

/ㅎ/ does not drop before the deferential ending, as in 노랗습니다, because the ending ~습니다 begins with a consonant. Observe more examples of these irregular adjectives.

Dictionary form		~습니다/ ㅂ니다	~어요/ 아요	~ㄴ/은	~세요/ 으세요
빨갛다	to be red	빨갛습니다	빨개요	빨간	—
하얗다	to be white	하얗습니다	하얘요	하얀	—
까맣다	to be black	까맣습니다	까매요	까만	—
이렇다	to be this way	이렇습니다	이래요	이런	이러세요
그렇다	to be so	그렇습니다	그래요	그런	그러세요
저렇다	to be that way	저렇습니다	저래요	저런	저러세요
어떻다	to be some way	어떻습니까	어때요	어떤	어떠세요

2. Some stems, such as 좋다, 많다, and 싫다 ('to be undesirable'), follow the regular pattern of conjugation: 좋습니다, 좋아요, 좋은.

Exercise

Conjugate the given dictionary forms according to the context.

(1) 저는 머리가 (좋다) <u>좋은</u> 사람하고 결혼하고 싶어요.

(2) 마크 눈은 (파랗다)_____ 색이에요.

(3) 동생이 머리가 (까맣다)_____.

(4) 그 남자는 (어떻다)_____ 사람이에요?

(5) 김 선생님이 (어떻다) _____?

(6) 요즘은 (많다)_____ 학생들이 한국어를 배워요.

G12.5   The noun-modifying form [Verb ~(으)ㄴ] + N (past)

(1) 어제 **먹은** 갈비가 맛있었어요.

The *galbi* that I ate yesterday was tasty.

(2) 스티브가 **입은** 옷은 아주 비싸요.

The clothes that Steve is wearing are very expensive.

(3) 어제 **만난** 친구를 오늘 또 만났어요.

Today I saw the friend again whom I (had) met yesterday.

✎   Notes

Notes

1. [Verb stem~(으)ㄴ] + N is the past form of a verb in relative clauses (noun-modifying constructions). Recall that when ~(으)ㄴ occurs with adjectives, it indicates a present situation (G9.2).

a. 민지가 **산** 차는 작아요.	The car that Minji **bought** is small.
b. 민지가 **작은** 차를 샀어요.	Minji bought a **small** car.

[~(으)ㄴ] + N, (a) when used with verbs, expresses past or completed actions or events (see G10.5 for the use of ~는 for present or ongoing action), but (b) when used with adjectives, expresses present situations.

2. When verbs for 'to wear, put on' occur with ~(으)ㄴ, they indicate the result of a past action. For example:

a.	[모자를 쓴] 사람은 우리 남동생이에요.	The person who wears a cap is my younger brother.
b.	[안경을 낀] 사람은 우리 형이에요.	The person who wears glasses is my older brother.

3. Conjugation of noun-modifying constructions:

	Verb	Adjective	있다/없다	이다
Past/ completed	(으)ㄴ	-	-	-
Present/ ongoing	는	(으)ㄴ	는	ㄴ
Prospective/ unrealized	(으)ㄹ	(으)ㄹ	을	ㄹ

Notice that past/complete suffixes do not occur with adjectives (including 있다/없다 and 이다).

Examples of conjugation:

	Verb	Adjective	있다/없다	이다
	읽다 가다	좋다 싸다	재미있다 맛없다	학생이다
Past/ completed	읽은 간	-	-	-
Present/ ongoing	읽는 가는	좋은 싼	재미있는 맛없는	학생인
Prospective/ unrealized	읽을 갈	좋을 쌀	재미있을 맛없을	학생일

Exercises

1. Underline the noun-modifying clause + Noun in each sentence below, and then translate the whole sentence into English as in (1).

(1) 이게 제가 지난 주에 <u>읽은 책</u>이에요.

   <u>This is the book that I read last week.</u>

(2) 이건 어제 마크한테서 받은 선물이에요.

   _____

(3) 우리 어머니가 만든 음식은 맛있어요.

   _____

(4) 지난 학기에 한국어를 가르치신 분은 이민수 선생님이에요.

   _____

(5) 스티브가 서울에서 찍은 사진들이 여기 있습니다.

   _____

(6) 키가 크고 안경을 낀 남자는 누구예요?

   _____

2. Change the verbs in the following noun-modifying clauses using the past-tense form ~(으)ㄴ, and then translate the clauses into English.

(1) 스티브가 **읽는** 책   the book (that) Steve reads

    스티브가 **읽은** 책   the book (that) Steve read

(2) 동생한테 주는 선물   _____

    _____

(3) 내가 듣는 음악   _____

    _____

(4) 마크가 쓰는 편지   _____

    _____

(5) 유미가 마시는 커피   _____

    _____

3. Make sentences using the noun-modifying clauses you made in exercise 2.

Example

스티브가 읽은 책

스티브가 읽은 책은 재미있었습니다.

Notes

. . . .

. . . .

. . . .

. . . .

. . . .

. . . .

Narration   가족 사진

우리 가족은 할머니, 아버지,
어머니, 누나, 형, 남동생, 나,
모두 일곱 명입니다. 여기 우리
가족 사진이 있습니다. 이 가족
사진은 작년 할머니 생신에 찍은
사진입니다. 가운데 노란 한복을 입고 계신 분이 할머니이십니다.
할머니는 연세가 많으신데 아주 건강하십니다. 할머니 뒤에
계신 분들이 우리 부모님이십니다. 키가 크고 안경을 낀 사람은
우리 형입니다. 형은 대학원에 다닙니다. 머리가 긴 여자는 우리
누나입니다. 누나는 지난 봄에 결혼해서 지금은 시카고에서 살고
있습니다. 파란 모자를 쓴 남자는 제 남동생입니다. 남동생은
지금 고등학교[1]에 다닙니다. 내년에 대학생이 됩니다.

1. 고등학교: high school

Exercises

1. Answer the following questions based on the narration.

   (1) 우진의 가족은 모두 몇 명입니까?
   (2) 이 가족 사진은 언제 찍은 것입니까?
   (3) 할머니는 무슨 옷을 입고 계십니까?
   (4) 형은 어떤 사람입니까?
   (5) 누나는 어떤 사람입니까?
   (6) 남동생은 어떤 사람입니까?

2. Ask your classmate to read the narration; then, based on what you hear,
draw a family photo with your book closed.

CULTURE

호칭 (Extending family terms to other social relations)

In contemporary Korean culture, some family terms are often extended to refer to social relations without blood ties. An elder male is addressed as 할아버지 (grandfather), an elder female as 할머니 (grandmother), a middle-aged male as 아저씨 (uncle), and a middle-aged female as 아주머니 (aunt).

Among group members of similar ages, terms referring to siblings are used. 언니 is a term used by a younger female to address an older female, while 오빠 is a term used by a younger female to address an older male. 누나 is used by a younger male to refer to an older female, while 형 is used by a younger male to refer to an older male.

To address the father of your friend, you can say 아버님, an honorific expression for "father." To address the mother of your friend, you can say either 어머님 or 어머니, both of which are honorific expressions for "mother."

USAGE

A Talking about family

가족	이름	나이	사는 곳 (residence)
할머니	김순아	75	로스앤젤레스
아버지	한갑수	53	로스앤젤레스
어머니	이남희	49	로스앤젤레스
누나	한유경	24	프린스턴
형	한준호	22	텍사스
나	한유진	20	서울
여동생	한미선	17	로스앤젤레스

Exercise 1

The chart above lists ages and places of residence for each of Yujin's family members. Work in pairs to exchange information on each of Yujin's family members.

Example: A: 유진 씨 할머니는 연세가 어떻게 되세요?
  B: 일흔 다섯이세요.
  A: 지금 어디 사세요?
  B: 로스앤젤레스에 사세요.

Exercise 2

Answer the following questions:

(1) 유진은 집에서 몇 째예요?
  (몇 째 [order of birth among siblings])
(2) 막내의 이름은 뭐예요?
(3) 아들이 몇 명 있어요? 딸은 몇 명이에요?
(4) 누나는 이름이 뭐예요? 어디서 살아요?
(5) 할머님 성함은 어떻게 되세요?

Exercise 3

Practice the following dialogue:

> A: 가족이 많으세요?
>
> B: 네, 할아버지, 아버지, 어머니, 언니, 오빠, 여동생, 나, 모두
>   7명이에요.
>
> A: 부모님은 어디 사세요?
>
> B: 보스턴에 사세요.
>
> A: 형제들은 다 어디 살아요?
>
> B: 오빠는 뉴욕에 살고, 언니는 하와이에 살고, 여동생은 보스턴에 살아요.

Now play the role of speaker B and describe your own family.

> A: 가족이 많으세요?
>
> B: 네, _____
>
>   (아니요, _____ 밖에 없어요.)
>
> A: 부모님은 어디 사세요?
>
> B: _____에 사세요.
>
> A: 형제들은 다 어디 살아요?
>
> B: _____

Exercise 4

Draw your family tree including your grandparents, parents, and siblings, and tell your classmates about the people on it.

B *Ordinal numbers*

For the order of lessons (lesson 1, lesson 2, etc.), Sino-Korean numbers are used: 일 과, 이 과, 삼 과, 사 과, and so on.

Exercise 1

Answer the following questions:

(1) 오늘 몇 과를 공부해요? _____

(2) 어제는 몇 과를 공부했어요? _____

(3) 내일 몇 과를 배워요? _____

Exercise 2

Using the images below, answer the questions.

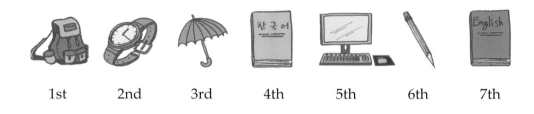

1st   2nd   3rd   4th   5th   6th   7th

(1) 사전이 어디 있어요?   <u>일곱 번째 박스('box')에 있어요.</u>

(2) 한국어 책은 어디 있어요?   _____

(3) 연필은 어디 있어요?   _____

(4) 가방은 어디 있어요?   _____

(5) 세 번째에는 뭐가 있어요?   _____

(6) 다섯 번째에는 뭐가 있어요?   _____

(7) 두 번째에는 뭐가 있어요?   _____

C *Describing clothes and colors*

Exercise 1

Describe the clothes the family members in the picture are wearing, as well as the non-clothing items they may have.

할머니는 한복을 <u>입으셨어요</u>.

아버지는 넥타이를 _____

어머니는 가방을 _____

형은 안경을 _____

동생은 모자를 _____

누나는 치마를 _____

Notice the difference between color adjectives and their conjugated forms.
우리 어머니 눈은 까만 색이에요. 어머니 머리도 까매요.

Exercise 2

Based on your own appearance, answer the following questions in Korean.

(1) 머리가 무슨 색이에요? _____

(2) 눈은 무슨 색깔이에요? _____

(3) 좋아하는 색이 뭐예요? _____

(4) 오늘 입은 옷 색깔이 뭐예요? _____

(5) 무슨 색 옷을 자주 입어요? _____

Lesson 12 Family

CONVERSATION 1   *Where are you from?*

Students introduce themselves in a classroom.

Mark: Minji, where are you from?

Minji: I'm from Vancouver in Canada. I was born and raised there.[G12.1]

Mark: Does your entire family live in Vancouver?

Minji: No, only my parents are there, and my siblings all live elsewhere.

Mark: Do you have a lot of siblings?

Minji: Yes, there's four including me. I'm the second oldest. I have one older brother and two younger siblings. Where does your family live, Mark?

Mark: My parents are in Sydney while my older brother is married and lives on the East Coast in the United States. My youngest sibling is studying in the U.K. and is coming to Seoul next week.

Minji: Ah, really? That must be nice.[G12.2]

CONVERSATION 2   *Your family picture came out [well] nice.*

Minji and Woojin talk about their families.

Minji: How old are your parents?

Woojin: My father is fifty-five and my mother is fifty-three. Here's our family picture, would you like to see it?

Minji: Wow, the picture really came out [well] nice![G12.3] When did you take this picture?

Woojin: We took it on my grandmother's birthday last year.

Minji: Is the person wearing the yellow hanbok[G12.4, G12.5] here your grandmother?

Woojin: Yes.

Minji: The tall person here is your older brother, right?

Woojin: Yes, he's my older brother. He's attending graduate school now.

Minji: Your eyes look like your older brother's.

NARRATION	*Family Picture*

Our family consists of 7 people: my grandmother, father, mother, older sister, older brother, younger brother, and me. Here is our family picture. This family picture was taken for my grandmother's birthday last year. The person in the center wearing the yellow hanbok is my grandmother. My grandmother is elderly, but she is very healthy. The people behind my grandmother are my parents. The tall person wearing glasses is my older brother. He attends graduate school. The woman with long hair is my older sister. She got married last spring and now lives in Chicago. The guy wearing the blue hat is my younger brother. He is currently in high school. He will be a college student next year.

13과 전화

Lesson 13 On the Telephone

Conversation 1   스티브 씨 좀 바꿔 주세요.

Soobin calls Steve to find out why he was absent.

Conversation   1

(따르릉 따르릉)

스티브: 여보세요.

수빈: 거기 스티브 씨 집이지요?

스티브: 네, 그런데요.

수빈: 스티브 씨 좀 바꿔 주세요.G13.1

스티브: 전데요. 실례지만 누구세요?

수빈: 저 김수빈이에요. 오늘 왜 학교에 안 왔어요?

스티브: 감기에 걸려서 못 갔어요.

수빈: 많이 아파요?

스티브: 아침엔 많이 아팠는데, 이젠 좀 괜찮아요.

수빈: 내일은 학교에 올 거예요?

스티브: 네, 시험이 있어서 가야 돼요.G13.2

수빈: 그래요? 그럼 몸조리 잘 하세요.

스티브: 네, 전화해 줘서 고마워요.

수빈: 그럼 또 전화할게요.G13.3

NEW WORDS

NOUN

도시	city
몸조리	care of health
엄마	mom

VERB

감기에 걸리다	to have/catch a cold
돕다	to help
바꾸다	to change, switch
빨래하다	to do the laundry
부치다	to mail (a letter, parcel)
비(가) 오다	to rain
빌리다	to borrow
빌려주다	to lend
실례하다	to be excused

ADJECTIVE

배(가) 고프다	to be hungry

ADVERB

나중에	later
다시	again
여보세요	hello (on the phone)
이따가	a little later
이젠	now (이제+는)

SUFFIX

~(으)ㄹ게요	I will (volition or promise)
~어/아 주다	do something for another's benefit
~어/아야 되다	must (obligation or necessity)

NEW EXPRESSIONS

1. 따르릉 따르릉 is an onomatopoeic expression denoting the telephone ring.

2. 여보세요 'hello' (for telephone) comes from 여기 보세요 'Look here'.

3. 실례지만 누구세요? 'Excuse me, but who is this?' 실례지만 'excuse me, but' can precede a question to express courtesy. Note that 'Excuse me' is 실례합니다.

저 . . . 실례지만 지금 몇 시예요?
저 . . . 실례지만 말씀 좀 묻겠습니다.

4. Both 지금 and 이제 (이젠) indicate the present moment of speech and can be translated as 'now'. However, the two expressions refer to the present moment in two different senses. 이제 involves a change in situation from the previous moments, whereas 지금 simply indicates the present moment without relating it to any other time.

5. 몸조리 잘 하세요 'Please take good care of yourself' is an idiomatic expression addressed to someone who is ill. 몸 is 'body' and 조리 is 'care of health, recuperation'.

6. Some telephone expressions:

전화번호	telephone number
여보세요.	Hello.
[person]한테 전화하세요.	Please call [a person].
전화해 주세요.	Please give me a call.
[person]한테서 전화가 오다.	The phone call is from [a person].
전화 받으세요.	Please answer the phone.
[person] 좀 바꿔 주세요.	May I speak to [a person]?
잠깐만 기다리세요.	Just a minute, please.
이따가 다시 전화할게요.	I will call you later.

7. Parts of the body:

얼굴	face
입술	lips
가슴	chest
등	back
키	height
머리	head/hair
눈	eye
귀	ear
코	nose
입	mouth
이	tooth
턱	chin
목	neck
어깨	shoulder
팔	arm
손	hand
배	stomach, abdomen
다리	leg

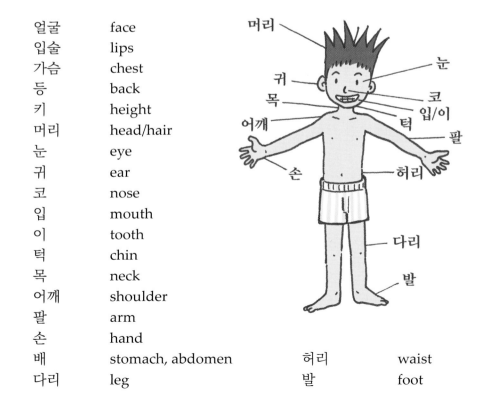

허리	waist
발	foot

Exercise

Complete the following telephone dialogue between Steve and Minji.

(Ring ring)

스티브: _____ (hello).

민지: _____ (hello).

        거기 스티브 씨 집이지요?

스티브: 네, 그런데요.

민지: 스티브 씨 있어요?

스티브: 전데요.

        _____(excuse me but . . .) 누구세요?

민지: 저 민지인데요. 오늘 수업에 왜 안 왔어요?

스티브: 감기에 _____ 못 갔어요.

        (I couldn't go because I had a cold.)

민지: 그래요? 그럼 몸조리 잘 하세요.

Grammar

G13.1   The benefactive expression ~어/아 주다

(1)   파티에 **와 주세요**.   Please come to the party.

(2)   엄마가 저한테 차를 **사 주셨어요.**   Mom bought me a car.

(3)   A: 제 전화 번호 알아요?   Do you know my phone number?

      B: 아니요, 번호 좀 **가르쳐 주세요.**   No, please let me have it.

(4)   **도와 주셔서** 감사합니다.   Thank you for helping (me).

Examples

Notes

1. 주다 as a main verb means 'to give', as in the following examples:

마이클이 리사한테 꽃을 주었어요.   선생님이 저한테 사전을 주셨어요.

The recipient is marked with the particle 한테 or 에게.

2. As an auxiliary verb, 주다 is used in the construction of [verb stem + ~어/아 주다] which means 'to do something for someone'. Compare the two sentences below:

    (a)   스티브가 책을 읽었어요.
    (b)   스티브가 동생한테 책을 읽어 주었어요.

Sentence (a) simply means that Steve read a book, but (b) means that Steve read a book to someone else.

[Verb stem + ~어/아 주다] takes the following forms:

사 주다	to buy for someone's benefit
읽어 주다	to read for someone's benefit
빌려 주다*	to lend for someone's benefit
도와 주다	to help for someone's benefit

    *빌려 주다 'to lend' (cf. 빌리다 'to borrow')

3. ~어/아 주세요 is also used when requesting something in which the benefit is for the speaker: "Please do . . . for me."

    a.   책을 읽으세요.   Read the book.
    b.   책을 (저한테) 읽어 주세요.   Please read the book (for me).

Both ~어/아 주세요 and ~(으)세요 can be used in making requests or commands. However, they differ in degree of politeness. ~어/아 주세요 is much more polite than ~(으)세요. Sentence (a) simply imposes some action on the listener, whereas (b) indicates that the speaker is making the request for his/her own benefit. When you are asking to speak to someone on the phone, ___ 씨 좀 바꾸세요 is not appropriate. Instead, use ____씨 좀 바꿔 주세요.

4. ~어/아 주셔서 감사합니다 is used to express gratitude. The adverb 대단히 'very much' can be added. 감사합니다 can be replaced with 고맙습니다.

생일 파티에 와 주셔서　　　Thank you for coming to my
감사합니다/고맙습니다.　　birthday party.

한국어를 가르쳐 주셔서　　Thank you for teaching me
감사합니다/고맙습니다.　　Korean.

Compare ~어/아 주다 with other sentence endings below. Notice that when the stem 주 is followed by ~어요, the contracted form 줘요 can be used.

Dictionary form	~어/아요	~(으)세요	~어/아 줘요	~어/아 주세요
오다	와요	오세요	와 줘요	와 주세요
가르치다	가르쳐요	가르치세요	가르쳐 줘요	가르쳐 주세요
읽다	읽어요	읽으세요	읽어 줘요	읽어 주세요
전화하다	전화해요	전화하세요	전화해 줘요	전화해 주세요
쓰다	써요	쓰세요	써 줘요	써 주세요
돕다	도와요	도우세요	도와 줘요	도와 주세요

Grammar

G13.2   Expressing obligation or necessity: ~어/아야 되다

(1)   매일 운동해**야 돼요**.   (We/I) have to exercise every day.

(2)   내일 아침 교수님하고   I have an appointment with my
      약속이 있어요.   professor tomorrow morning.
      일찍 일어나**야 돼요**.   I have to get up early.

(3)   A: 이번 주말에 바빠요?
      B: 네, 집 청소하고 빨래해**야 돼요**.

(4)   A: 오후에 뭐 할 거예요?
      B: 도서관에 가서 책을 빌려**야 돼요**.

Notes

1. ~어/아야 되다 and its alternative form ~어/아야 하다 express the idea of obligation or necessity. ~어/아야 하다 sounds slightly more formal than ~어/아야 되다.

학생은 열심히 공부해야 돼요.   Students must study hard.
                                         (colloquial)
학생은 열심히 공부해야 해요.   Students must study hard.
                                         (slightly formal)

2. ~어/아야 되다 and ~어/아야 하다 occur in the following forms:

좋다	좋아야 돼요/해요	have to be good
가다	가야 돼요/해요	have to go
먹다	먹어야 돼요/해요	have to eat
모자를 쓰다	모자를 써야 돼요/해요	have to wear a hat
조용하다	조용해야 돼요/해요	have to be quiet

Exercises

1. Change the verbs in parentheses to express necessity by using ~어/아야 되다.

   (1) 비가 와요. 우산을 (사다) <u>사야 돼요</u>.

   (2) 엄마한테 편지를 (부치다) _____.

   (3) 도시에서는 차가 많이 막혀서 지하철을 (타다) _____.

   (4) 돈이 없어요. 일을 (하다) _____.

   (5) 다음 학기에는 심리학 수업을 (듣다) _____.

   (6) 룸메이트를 찾아요. 그런데 학생 (이다) _____.

2. Tell your class what you need to do this week, using ~어/아야 되다 as in the example.

월요일:	시험	월요일에는 시험을 봐야 돼요.
화요일:	수업	_____
수요일:	한국어 숙제	_____
목요일:	친구	_____
금요일:	생일 파티	_____
토요일:	집 청소	_____

/ **Notes**

Grammar

G13.3 The sentence ending ~(으)ㄹ게요

(1) A: 전화 왔는데 제가 받을까요?   The telephone is ringing;
                                              shall I answer it?

     B: 괜찮아요. 제가 **받을게요**.   It's all right. I will answer it.

(2) A: 지금 시간 있으세요?   Do you have time now?
     B: 지금 좀 바쁜데요.   I'm a little busy now.
     A: 그럼, 이따가 다시 **올게요**.   Then I will come again later.

Notes

1. The sentence ending ~(으)ㄹ게요 expresses the speaker's willingness, assurance, or promise to do something for the listener's sake. This form can be used only in statements, not in questions. The subject must be in the first person.

2. Compare ~(으)ㄹ게요 and ~(으)ㄹ래요 (G11.2). Neither ~(으)ㄹ게요 nor ~(으)ㄹ래요 allows a third person to be the subject of the sentence. Unlike ~(으)ㄹ게요, ~(으)ㄹ래요 can be used in questions, in which case the listener's intention can be used in questions to ask for the listener's intention.

3. While ~(으)ㄹ게요 denotes willingness, assurance, or promise, ~(으)ㄹ래요 denotes intention and assertion. Compare these examples:

교실에서

선생님: 누가 책을 읽을래요?   Who will read the book?
스티브: 제가 읽을게요.   I will read it. (volunteering)
마크: 아니에요, 제가 읽을래요.   No, I will read it. (asserting)

식당에서

A:	뭐 드시겠어요?	What would you like to eat?
B:	저는 갈비 먹을게요.	I'd like to have *kalbi*. (modest, guest-like)
C:	저는 불고기 먹을래요.	I will have *bulgogi*. (asserting)

Exercise

Complete the following dialogue by conjugating the verbs using the ~(으)ㄹ게요 form.

(1) A: 내일 몇 시에 만날까요?

     B: 제가 오늘 밤에 (전화하다) <u>전화할게요</u>.

(2) A: 숙제를 하는데 너무 어려워요.

     B: 제가 도와 (주다) _____.

(3) A: 오늘 집에 일찍 오세요.

     B: 네, 일찍 (오다) _____.

(4) A: 지금 커피 마실래요?

     B: 아니에요. 괜찮아요. 나중에 (마시다) _____.

(5) A: 음식이 없어요. 누가 장보러 갈래요?

     B: 제가 (가다) _____.

Notes

Conversation 2   박 교수님 연구실이지요?

▌Mark calls Professor Park, and a graduate student answers the phone.

Conversation   2

         (따르릉 따르릉)

대학원생: 여보세요.

마크: 여보세요. 거기 박 교수님 연구실이지요?

대학원생: 네, 그런데요.

마크: 박 교수님 좀 부탁합니다.

대학원생: 네, 잠깐만 기다리세요.

              교수님, 전화 왔습니다.

박 교수님: 여보세요. 전화 바꿨습니다.

마크: 안녕하세요, 교수님. 저 마크 스미스입니다.

              한국어 수업 때문에[G13.4] 좀 뵙고 싶은데

              내일 학교에 나오세요?

박 교수님: 네, 오후 2시부터 4시까지 연구실에 있을 거예요.

마크: 그럼 2시 반에 연구실로 가겠습니다.[G13.5]

박 교수님: 그럼 내일 봐요.

마크: 네, 안녕히 계세요.

NEW WORDS

NOUN

그동안	meantime
뉴스	news
메시지	message
물가	cost of living
반	half (e.g., 30 min)
발	foot
비	rain
신발	shoes
인터뷰	interview

PRE-NOUN

새	new

ADJECTIVE

시끄럽다	to be noisy

VERB

남기다	to leave (a message)
돈이 들다	to cost money
들어가다	to enter
부탁하다	to ask a favor

ADVERB

그만	without doing anything further
때문에	because of
잠깐만	for a short time

SUFFIX

~겠	② would (intention)

NEW EXPRESSIONS

1. . . . 좀 부탁합니다 (*lit.* I would like to ask you a favor) is used in telephone conversations to ask "May I speak to . . . ?"

2. 전화 바꿨습니다 (*lit.* I switched the telephone) is a standard expression to report to the caller that the requested person has taken over the receiver from another person.

3. 좀 뵙고 싶은데요 'I would like to see you' is used only to a senior person or a distant adult.

Exercise

Make up a telephone dialogue with your partner by changing the underlined portions of the example.

(1) A: 여보세요, 거기 학교 사무실이지요?

    B: 네, 그런데요.

    A: <u>이민수 씨</u> 좀 부탁합니다.

    B: 실례지만 누구세요?

    A: 네, [your name]인데요.

    B: 잠깐만 기다리세요.

(2) 꽃집/ 김상호

(3) 커피숍/ 이미진

(4) 극장/ 신성희

(5) 연구실/ 박영진 교수님

(6) 서울은행/ 장윤진

(7) 마크 씨 집/ 마크

Grammar

G13.4   Noun 때문에

(1) A: 그동안 어떻게 지내셨어요?

    B: 한국어 수업 **때문에** 좀 바빴어요.

(2) A: 룸메이트 **때문에** 못 잤어요.   I couldn't sleep because of
                                          my roommate.

    B: 피곤하겠어요.

(3) 감기 **때문에** 어제 집에 일찍 들어갔어요.

Examples

Notes

1. The word 때문 means 'reason'. It cannot be used by itself, but must be preceded by a noun or noun phrase. With a preceding noun and the particle 에, the construction [Noun 때문에] expresses a causal relationship as in 'because of'.

2. After [Noun 때문에] the main predicate may be omitted to avoid repetition.

> A: 한국에 왜 가세요?
>
> B: 일 때문에 가요 or 일 때문에요.

Exercises

1. Make complete sentences using 때문에, as shown in the example.

(1) 숙제 / 시간이 없어요.　　　　숙제 때문에 시간이 없어요.

(2) 한국어 수업 / 학교에 일찍 와요.　_____

(3) 비 / 차가 많이 막혔어요.　_____

(4) 여자친구 / 돈이 많이 들어요.　_____

(5) 작은 신발 / 발이 아파요.　_____

(6) 인터뷰 / 새 옷을 샀어요.　_____

2. Answer the following questions using the [Noun 때문에] or [Noun 때문에요] construction.

(1) 요즘 왜 바쁘세요?　　　　　　[시험]

(2) 왜 기숙사에서 나왔어요?　　　[시끄러운 룸메이트]

(3) 왜 머리가 아파요?　　　　　　[감기]

(4) 어제 왜 학교에 안 왔어요?　　[한국에서 온 친구]

(5) 왜 돈이 많이 들어요?　　　　　[비싼 물가]

G13.5   Intentional ~겠~

(1) 저는 내일 가**겠**습니다.   I will go tomorrow.

(2) A: 뭐 마시**겠**어요?   What would you like to
                                                drink?

     B: 커피 마실게요.   I would like coffee.

(3) A: 누가 책을 읽**겠**어요?   Who will read the book?
     B: 제가 읽**겠**습니다.   I will read it.

(4) A: 거기 이 선생님 계세요?
     B: 지금 안 계시는데요. 메시지를 남기**겠**습니까?

    Notes

1. ~겠~, which indicates conjecture (G12.2), can also be used to express the
speaker's intention or volition, and can be glossed as 'will'. In speech,
~(으)ㄹ래요 usually replaces intentional ~겠~ which cannot be preceded by the
past-tense suffix ~었/았 while conjectural ~겠~ (G12.2) can. Intentional ~겠~
indicates the speaker's intention or volition in statements and probes for that
of the listener in questions.

   Statements:
   제가 가겠어요.   I will go.
   내일 다시 오겠어요.   I will come again tomorrow.

   On the street
   말씀 좀 묻겠습니다.   May I ask you something?
                                        (*lit.* I will ask you something.)

   Greeting
   처음 뵙겠습니다.   Nice to meet you. (*lit.* I'm meeting
                                        you for the first time.)

   Questions:
   At a restaurant
   뭐 드시겠어요?   What would you like to eat?

2. In addition, ~겠~ occurs in idiomatic expressions in the following contexts:

Saying good-bye
그만 가 보겠습니다.　　　See you later.
　　　　　　　　　　　(*lit.* I'll be leaving now.)

Before a meal
잘 먹겠습니다.　　　　　I will enjoy the meal.
　　　　　　　　　　　(*lit.* I will eat well.)

In a classroom
시험을 시작하겠습니다.　We will begin the exam.

Weather forecast
내일은 비가 오겠습니다.　It will rain tomorrow.

News report
지금부터 뉴스를　　　　The news will start now.
시작하겠습니다.

Exercise

Translate the following sentences using ~겠~.

(1) (On the street) May I ask you something?

　　　_____

(2) Nice to meet you.

　　　_____

(3) A: Who will read lesson 11?

　　　_____

　　 B: I will read it.

　　　_____

(4) (To a professor) I will go to your office tomorrow at 9 o'clock.

　　　_____

Narration · 전화 메시지

1. Steve leaves a voice message on Mark's phone.

마크 씨, 안녕하세요? 저 스티브 윌슨인데요.
한국어 숙제 때문에 전화했어요. 내일 아침
10시에 학교 도서관 앞에서 만나고 싶은데
시간 괜찮아요? 저한테 전화 좀 해 주세요.
제 전화 번호는 512-6094예요. 안녕히 계세요.

2. Minji leaves a voice message on her mom's phone.

엄마, 저 민지예요. 그동안 잘 지내셨지요?
저는 학교에 잘 다니고 있어요. 저 . . .
책을 사야 되는데 지난 달에 받은 돈을 다
썼어요. 서울은 물가가 비싸서 돈이 굉장히
많이 들어요. 죄송하지만 은행으로 돈 좀
보내 주세요. 오백 불만 부쳐 주세요. 엄마,
고맙습니다.

Exercises

1. Fill in the blanks based on the narration.

    (1) 스티브는 _____ 때문에 마크한테 전화했습니다.

    (2) 스티브의 _____는 512-6094입니다.

    (3) 민지는 _____ 때문에 엄마한테 전화했습니다.

    (4) 민지는 _____ 되는데 돈이 없습니다.

    (5) 민지 엄마가 민지한테 오백 불을 _____ 주실 겁니다.

2. Fill in the blanks with appropriate particles (이/가 or 을/를)

    (1) 유미는 돈_____ 많아요.

    (2) 우진은 어제 백화점에서 돈_____ 많이 썼어요.

    (3) 서울에서는 돈_____ 많이 들어요.

    (4) 마크는 서점에서 돈_____ 벌어요 ('to earn money').

Notes

CULTURE

축구, 야구, 씨름, 그리고 태권도 (Soccer, baseball, Ssireum, and Taekwondo)

Like people in many other countries all around the world, Koreans enjoy diverse sports. Soccer is one of the most popular sports in Korea.

Korean traditional sports, on the other hand, represent other values and meanings besides popularity. 씨름, for example, is a sport of the traditional holidays. It is a kind of wrestling where two people compare their strength and skills in a sand ring. Anyone who touches the ground with a part of their body other than their feet loses the game. Usually, the winner of the competition is awarded a miniature golden bull. 태권도 is another traditional sport that is widely practiced in Korea. As more of a traditional martial art rather than a popular sport, it is valued as a way to train one's body and spirit. Many people learn it from childhood, and men are trained in it once again when they join the military.

Some Korean athletes have been internationally recognized for their talents. At the 2010 Winter Olympics 김연아 (Yuna Kim) became the first Korean to win the gold medal in figure skating and broke the record for the amount of points she received for her routine.

USAGE

A　*Making telephone calls*

Both the caller and the person called say 여보세요 'hello' when the call is made. To confirm that he or she has dialed the right number, the caller usually asks a question—"Is this Mr. Lee's residence?" "Is this Professor Kim's office?" or the like. This kind of question is often in the ~지요? form as in the following examples:

A:	여보세요.	Hello.
B:	여보세요.	Hello.
A:	거기 [김 교수님 연구실]이지요?	Is this [Professor Kim's office]?
B:	네, 그런데요.	Yes, it is.
A:	[교수님] 좀 부탁합니다.	May I speak to
	(=[교수님] 좀 바꿔 주세요.)	[Professor Kim]?
B:	네, 잠깐만 기다리세요.	Just a minute, please.

 Exercise 1

Practice the preceding dialogue by substituting the following for the expressions in brackets.

(1) 한국 은행 / 김민호 씨

(2) 꽃집 / 홍수미 씨

(3) 서울 약국 / 박철수 씨

(4) *마이클네 집 / 마이클

　　　(*마이클네 집 'the house of Michael's family')

More telephone expressions:

지금 없는데요.	He/she is not here now.
(honorific form: 지금 안 계신데요)	
이따가 다시 전화할게요.	I will call again later.
통화 중이에요.	The line is busy.

Exercise 2

Read the following telephone numbers.

(1)   431-7890

(2)   136-0210

(3)   667-8903

(4)   445-7021

Exercise 3

Ask several classmates their telephone numbers, using the following example as a model.

린다: 샌디 씨, 전화 번호가 뭐예요?

샌디: 947의 6981이에요.

Exercise 4

Ask your teacher's telephone number.

학생: 선생님 연구실 전화 번호가 어떻게 되세요?

선생님: 932의 5603이에요.

Exercise 5

Practice speaking with a classmate using the following situations.

(1) You call your girlfriend/boyfriend. She/he is not at home and her/his father asks who is calling. Politely leave your name and tell him that you will call later.

(2) You call Professor Kim's residence and his wife picks up the phone. She says that Professor Kim is not there.

B *Making an appointment*

To make an appointment for some specific purpose, you can indicate that purpose as follows:

[purpose] 때문에 좀 뵙고 싶은데요 / 만나고 싶은데요.

뵙고 싶은데요 is used to refer to someone higher in social status or older than you are. If you and the person you would like to see are peers, 만나고 싶은데요 is used.

지난 번에 본 시험 때문에 좀 뵙고 싶은데요.
스티브 씨, 숙제 때문에 좀 만나고 싶은데요.

To set a time or date, you can use the following expressions:

무슨 요일이 좋아요?   What day is good for you?
몇 시가 좋아요?   What time is good for you?

You can also suggest a time or date as follows:

[date/day/time] 괜찮으세요?/괜찮아요?   Is . . . okay with you?
                 어떠세요?/어때요?   How about . . . ?
                 좋으세요?/좋아요?   Is . . . good for you?
          A: 교수님, 숙제 때문에 좀 뵙고 싶은데요.
                내일 연구실에 계실 거예요?
          B: 네, 1시부터 있을 거예요.
          A: 그럼, 2시 어떠세요?
          B: 2시 괜찮아요.
          A: 그럼 내일 2시에 뵙겠습니다.

Exercise

Practice the following situation with a classmate:
Call your professor and ask for a makeup test. Give a reason why you couldn't take the test. Make an appointment with the professor for a specific date and time.

C   *Describing illness or pain*

A: 어디가 아프세요?   Where does it hurt?

B: [Part of the body]이/가 아파요.

머리가 아파요   to have a headache

목이 아파요   to have a sore throat

이가 아파요   to have a toothache

배가 아파요   to have a stomachache

감기 걸렸어요   to have caught a cold

열이 나요   to have a fever

몸이 안 좋아요   to not feel well

Exercise

Practice the following conversation, and then substitute the conditions indicated by the pictures for the underlined part below.

A: 저는 몸('body')이 안 좋아서 파티에 못 가요.

B: 어디가 아프세요?

A: <u>이가 아파요</u>.

B: 많이 아프세요?

A: 이젠 좀 괜찮아요.

(1)   (2)   (3)

(4)   (5)

D *Making a polite request/question*

실례지만 'Excuse me but, . . .' or 실례합니다 'Excuse me' is used to show politeness before you ask a question. Typical uses of 실례지만 include asking directions on the street or confirming a telephone number you have just dialed.

Examples

(1) On the street:

> A: 실례지만 말씀 좀 묻겠습니다.
>
> Excuse me, but may I ask you something?
>
> B: 네.
>
> Yes.

(2) On the telephone:

> A: 실례지만 김 교수님 좀 바꿔 주시겠습니까?
>
> Excuse me, but is Professor Kim there?
>
> B: 지금 안 계신데요.
>
> No, he is not here.

(3) Office visit:

> A: 저 . . . 여기가 김 교수님 연구실입니까?
>
> Is this Professor Kim's office?
>
> B: 네. 그런데요. 실례지만 무슨 일로 오셨어요?
>
> Yes, it is. How can I help you?

Exercise

Using 실례지만, ask your classmate

(1) how old she or he is.

(2) whether he/she has a boyfriend/girlfiend.

(3) where he/she bought the clothes that she/he is wearing.

(4) what size shoes he/she is wearing.

Lesson 13 On the Telephone

CONVERSATION 1 *May I speak to Steve?*

Soobin calls Steve to find out why he was absent.

(Ring ring)

Steve:	Hello.
Soobin:	Is this Steve's house?
Steve:	Yes, it is.
Soobin:	May I please speak to Steve?[G13.1]
Steve:	Speaking. Who is this, may I ask?
Soobin:	It's me, Soobin Kim. Why didn't you come to school today?
Steve:	I couldn't go because I caught a cold.
Soobin:	Are you very sick?
Steve:	I was very sick in the morning, but I'm okay now.
Soobin:	Are you coming to school tomorrow?
Steve:	Yes, I have an exam so I have to.[G13.2]
Soobin:	Really? Okay then, take care of yourself.
Steve:	I will, thank you for calling.
Soobin:	Well then, I'll call you again later.[G13.3]

CONVERSATION 2 *Is this Professor Park's residence?*

Mark calls Professor Park, and a graduate student answers the phone.

(Ring ring)

Graduate student:	Hello.
Mark:	Hello. Is this Professor Park's office?
Graduate student:	Yes, it is.
Mark:	May I please speak to Professor Park?
Graduate student:	Yes, please wait a moment. Professor, you have a phone call.
Professor Park:	Hello. This is Professor Park speaking.
Mark:	Hello Professor. This is Mark Smith. I'd like to meet with you (to discuss something) regarding our Korean class.[G13.4] Are you coming to school tomorrow?
Professor Park:	Yes, I'll be in my office from 2 to 4 p.m.
Mark:	Then I'll go to your office at 2:30.[G13.5]
Professor Park:	See you tomorrow, then.
Mark:	Okay, good-bye.

NARRATION   *Phone message*

Steve leaves a voice message on Mark's phone.

Mark, hello. It's me, Steve Wilson. I called about the Korean homework. I'd like to meet at 10 o'clock tomorrow morning in front of the school library; is that time okay for you? Please give me a call. My phone number is 512-7094. Good-bye.

Minji leaves a voice message on her mom's phone.

Mom, it's me, Minji. How have you been? I'm doing well in school. Umm . . . I have to buy some books but I used all of the money I received last month. Things are expensive in Seoul so it takes quite a lot of money to live here. I'm sorry but can you please send some money through the bank? Just five hundred dollars, please. Thank you mom!

14과 공항에서

Lesson 14 At the Airport

Conversation 1   토요일이라서 길이 막히네요.

Mark takes a taxi to Incheon International Airport.

Conversation 1

기사: 어디까지 가세요?

마크: 인천 공항까지 가 주세요.

          오늘은 길이 많이 막히네요.

기사: 토요일이라서^{G14.1} 그래요.

마크: 공항까지 얼마나 걸릴까요?

          30분쯤 걸릴까요?

기사: 글쎄요, 그렇게 빨리 가지는 못 할^{G14.2} 거예요.

          적어도 한 시간은 걸리겠는데요.

마크: 네, 알겠습니다.

          (At the airport)

기사: 손님, 공항 다 왔어요.

마크: 아저씨, 얼마 나왔어요?

기사: 79,000원입니다.

마크: 여기 있습니다.

기사: 네, 감사합니다.

마크: 수고하세요.

NEW WORDS

NOUN		ADVERB	
공항	airport	적어도	at least
기사	driver	빨리	fast, quickly
길	street, road	**VERB**	
모레	the day after tomorrow	건너다	to cross
손님	guest, customer	(돈을) 내다	to pay
아저씨	mister; a man of one's parents' age	수고하다	to put forth effort, take trouble
안부	regards	운전하다	to drive (a car)
연락	contact	전하다	to give (regards)
인천	Incheon	**SUFFIX**	
전	before	~(이)라서	because Noun am/are/is
후	after		
휴일	holiday, day off	~지 못하다	cannot (long form of negation)

NEW EXPRESSIONS

1. 어디까지 가세요? (*lit.* How far are you going?) is used instead of 어디 가세요? 'Where are you going?' to emphasize the final destination.

2. In 토요일이라서 그래요 (*lit.* Because it is Saturday, it is like that.), the predicate 그래요 refers to the previous statement, 길이 많이 막히네요.

3. 다 왔어요 (*lit.* Came all the way.) is often used to express that someone has arrived at the destination.

4. 얼마 나왔어요? 'How much did the bill come out to?' refers to the fare shown on the taxi meter.

5. 기사 literally refers to a person trained in engineering or architecture.

6. 수고하셨습니다 'Thanks for your trouble' can be used to a taxi driver when you get out of the taxi. These expressions are usually avoided when speaking to a hierarchical superior.

Exercises

1. Fill in the blanks with appropriate words.

   (1) _____에서 비행기를 타요.
   (2) 택시를 운전하는 사람은 _____예요.
   (3) 돈을 내고 택시를 타는 사람은 _____이에요.
   (4) 내일 다음은 _____예요.
   (5) _____에는 수업도 없고 일도 안 해요.

2. Fill in the blanks by spelling out the price of each item.

   | 5,700원 | 25,000원 | 116,000원 | 14,000원 |

   (1) 바지는 _____ 원이에요.
   (2) 사전은 _____ 원이에요.
   (3) 커피는 _____ 원이에요.
   (4) 가방은 _____ 원이에요.

3. Complete the following dialogue between a customer and a cab driver.

   기사: _____까지 가세요?
   마크: 공항이요. 공항까지 얼마나 _____?
   기사: 글쎄요, _____(at least two hours)은
            걸리겠는데요.
   기사: 손님, 다 왔어요.
   마크: _____? (How much is it?)
   기사: 32,000 원입니다.
   마크: 여기 있습니다.
            _____ (Thank you for your trouble.)
   기사: 감사합니다.

Grammar

G14.1 Noun~(이)라서 'because it is N'

Examples

(1) A: 지난 학기 잘 보냈어요? How was your semester?

B: 첫 학기**라서** 좀 바빴어요. Because it was my first semester, I was a little busy.

(2) A: 공항까지 얼마나 걸릴까요? How long (do you think) will it take to get to the airport?

B: 30분 후부터 길이 막히는 시간**이라서** 오래 걸릴 거예요. Because it is rush hour in 30 minutes, I guess it will take a long time.

Notes

1. The pattern [Clause 1~어서/아서 + Clause 2] is used to explain the cause of the event in clause 2 (G10.4). When ~어서/아서 occurs with [N이다] 'to be', it becomes [Noun~(이)라서]. 이라서 occurs after a noun ending in a consonant, and 라서 occurs after a noun ending in a vowel.

Noun(이)다	Noun~(이)라서	
학생이다	학생이라서	because someone is/was a student
겨울이다	겨울이라서	because it is/was winter
교수다	교수라서	because someone is/was a professor
의사다	의사라서	because someone is/was a doctor

2. The negative form of [Noun~(이)라서] is [Noun이/가 아니라서].

학생이 아니라서	교수가 아니라서
의사가 아니라서	겨울이 아니라서

Exercise

Complete the following dialogues, using the form N(이)라서.

(1) A: 오늘 왜 길에 차가 없어요?

     B: [holiday] 휴일이라서 그래요.

(2) A: 왜 운전을 안 하세요?

     B: [15 years old] _____ 운전을 아직 못 해요.

(3) A: 왜 한국어를 배우세요?

     B: 여자 친구가 [Korean]_____ 한국어를 배워요.

(4) A: 돈이 많으세요?

     B: 아니요. 저는 [student]_____ 돈이 없어요.

(5) A: 오늘 날씨가 참 따뜻하지요?

     B: 네, [spring]_____ 따뜻해요.

Grammar

G14.2   The negative ~지 못하다

Examples

(1) A: 내일 수영하러 가세요?   Are you going to go
                                           swimming tomorrow?

     B: 아니요, 바빠서 주말   No, since I'm busy,
           전에는 가**지 못할** 거예요.   I won't be able to do that
                                           before the weekend.

(2) 그동안 연락 드리**지 못해서**   I am very sorry for not
     (= 연락 못 드려서) 정말   having been able to contact
     죄송합니다. 할머니께   you for some time. Please
     안부 전해 주세요.   give my regards to
                                         grandmother.

(3) 일이 많아서 쉬**지 못하는**   There are holidays without
     휴일도 있습니다.   rest for me because I have
                                         lots of work to do.

Notes

[못 + Verb] indicates inability to do something (G6.4). The construction [verb stem~지 못하다] expresses the same notion in general. Verb stem~지 못하다 is slightly more formal than [못 + Verb].

Exercise

Change the following sentences using ~지 못하다.

(1) 배가 아파서 음식을 못 먹어요.

(2) 시간이 없어서 숙제를 못 했어요.

(3) 감기에 걸려서 일하러 못 갔어요.

(4) 미국에 간 스티브한테서 아직 연락을 못 받았어요.

(5) 모레는 수업이 있어서 파티에 못 갈 거예요.

(6) 돈이 없어서 전화비('phone bill')를 아직 못 냈어요.

(7) 차가 너무 많아서 길을 못 건너겠어요.

Notes

Conversation 2   마중 나왔어요.

Mark runs into Soobin at the airport.

Conversation 2

마크: 어, 수빈 씨, 여기 웬일이세요?

수빈: 마크 씨, 안녕하세요? 큰아버지 마중 나왔어요.
마크 씨는 공항에 웬일이세요?

마크: 오늘 영국에서 여동생이 와서 마중 나왔어요.

수빈: 아, 그래요? 몇 시 비행기인데요?

마크: 3시 비행기인데 제가 좀 늦게[G14.3] 도착했어요.

수빈: 공항까지 뭐 타고 오셨는데요?

마크: 택시 탔어요.

수빈: 택시비 많이 나왔겠네요.
다음에는 택시를 타지 마세요.[G14.4]

마크: 아, 몰랐어요.[G14.5]
다음에는 공항 버스를 타야 되겠네요.
공항 버스는 어디서 타요?

수빈: 출구 바로 앞에 정류장이 있어요.

NEW WORDS

NOUN

게임	game
계단	stairs
곳	place
노래방	karaoke (bar)
목소리	voice
엘리베이터	elevator
웬일	what matter
정류장	(bus) stop
출구	exit
큰아버지	uncle (father's older brother)
택시비	taxi fare
휴게실	lounge

ADVERB

더	more

ADJECTIVE

배(가) 부르다	to have a full stomach
적다	to be few, scarce

VERB

(노래) 부르다	to sing
도착하다	to arrive
마중 나오다/ 마중 나가다	to come/go out to greet someone
목(이) 마르다	to be thirsty
졸다	to doze off

SUFFIX

~게	adverbial suffix
~지 말다 (마세요)	to stop, cease

NEW EXPRESSIONS

1. 마중 나오다/나가다 means 'to come/go to a place (e.g., an airport) to greet/meet someone'. 마중 means 'receiving or meeting someone'.

2. 웬일이세요? [웬니리세요] 'What brings you here?, What are you doing here?' shows surprise when you see an acquaintance unexpectedly.

3. 택시비 'taxi fare' is a combination of the noun 택시 'taxi' and the morpheme 비 'cost', which can be used with other nouns as shown in the following:

전화비	telephone expenses	기숙사비	dormitory fee
버스비	bus fare	차비	transit fare

Exercises

1. Fill in the blanks with appropriate expressions.

    (1)　버스는 _____에서 타요.

    (2)　비행기가 20분 후에 _____ 거예요.

    (3)　택시를 타서 _____가 많이 나왔어요.

    (4)　_____는 아버지의 형이에요.

    (5)　공항에 _____ 나온 사람들이 많았어요.

    (6)　지하철에서 내려서 _____로 나가세요.

2. Match the most appropriate response from the right column to the question from the left column. Practice the conversation after the match is done.

(1)	(우체국에서) 여기 웬일이세요?	・　　　・	공항까지 가주세요.
(2)	얼마 나왔어요?	・　　　・	바빠서 택시 타고 왔어요.
(3)	공항까지 택시를 탈까요?	・　　　・	편지 부치러 왔어요.
(4)	버스를 어디서 타요?	・　　　・	이만 칠천 원 나왔습니다.
(5)	(택시 안) 어디까지 가세요?	・　　　・	출구로 나가서 길을 건너세요.
(6)	여기까지 뭐 타고 왔어요?	・　　　・	택시 타지 마세요.

Grammar

G14.3   The adverbial form ~게

(1) A: 오늘 수업에 왜 늦었어요?   Why were you late for class today?

B: 늦**게** 일어났어요.   I got up late.

(2) 잘 못 들었어요. 크**게** 말해 주세요.   I couldn't hear it. Please speak loud(ly).

(3) 저녁을 아주 맛있**게** 먹었어요.

(4) 크리스마스 즐겁**게** 보내세요.

Notes

The adverbial form ~게 refers to the manner or way in which something happens. ~게 is usually added to an adjective stem.

Adjective	Stem + ~게	Examples
바쁘다	바쁘게	지난 주말은 아주 바쁘게 보냈습니다.
시끄럽다	시끄럽게	도서관에서 시끄럽게 얘기하지 마세요.
적다	적게	이번 달은 전화비가 적게 나왔어요.

Exercise

Fill in the blanks with an appropriate adverbial form from the box below.

바쁘게   어렵게   싸게   재미있게   크게

(1) 일주일 전에 친구하고 영화를 _____ 봤어요.

(2) 목소리가 너무 작아요. 더 _____ 말해 주세요.

(3) 지난 주는 시험이 세 개나 있어서 _____ 지냈어요.

(4) A: 이 우산 얼마예요?

    B: _____ 드릴게요. 5,000원만 주세요.

(5) A: 시험 잘 봤어요?

    B: 아니요, 시험이 너무 _____ 나왔어요.
       그래서 잘 못 봤어요.

G14.4 Negative commands ~지 마세요

Examples

(1) (Speaker A offers a ride to his friend B, who is coming to visit Korea.)

A:	제가 공항에 마중 나갈게요.	I'll go out to the airport to greet you.
B:	복잡한데 나오**지 마세요**.	It's too crowded, so please don't come out to meet me.

(2)

A:	택시를 탈까요?	
B:	택시 타**지 말고** 지하철로 가세요.	Don't take a taxi. Take the subway instead.

(3) 수업 시간에 졸**지 마세요**.   Don't doze during the class.

(4) 비가 오는데 운전하**지 마세요**.   It is raining; don't drive.

Notes

1. Prohibition is expressed by ~지 마세요, consisting of two components: negation suffix ~지 and the verb 말다 'to stop (doing) something'. 마세요 is the honorific form of the verb 말다, a verb with an irregular ending with /ㄹ/. /ㄹ/ drops before /ㄴ/, /ㅂ/, and /ㅅ/.

2. When you want to express the idea 'Please don't do X, but instead do Y', use the construction [X~지 말고 Y~(으)세요].

수업 시간에 얘기하지 말고　　　Please don't talk during
선생님 말씀을 잘 들으세요.　　　class, but listen to the teacher.

커피 마시지 말고 주스 마셔요.　Please don't drink coffee but juice.

Exercises

1. Make up sentences using ~지 마세요.

(1)

(2)

(3)

(4)

(5)

(6)

2. Complete the following sentences using the ~지 말고 form.

(1) 텔레비전을 <u>보지 말고</u> 공부하세요.

(2) 엘리베이터를 ＿＿＿＿＿＿＿ 계단으로 내려가세요.

(3) 시험을 내일 ＿＿＿＿＿＿ 모레 보세요.

(4) 저녁에는 커피를 ＿＿＿＿＿＿ 주스를 드세요.

(5) 친구를 학교 식당에서 ＿＿＿＿＿＿ 휴게실에서 만나세요.

(6) 한국어 수업 시간에는 영어를 ＿＿＿＿＿＿ 한국어를 쓰세요.

G14.5   Irregular predicates in 르

Examples

(1) A: 한인타운에 가고 싶은데   I want to go to Koreatown.
       지하철이 **빨라**요?   Is the subway fast?
    B: 택시가 더 **빠른**데요.   A taxi would be faster.

(2) A: 더 드세요.   Please have some more.
    B: 아니요, 배가 **불러**서   No, I am too full and I
       못 먹겠어요.   can't eat any more.

(3) A: 뭐 타고 왔어요?   How did you come to
                                     school?
    B: 길을 잘 **몰라**서   I took a taxi because I didn't
       택시 타고 왔어요.   know the way.

🔊   **Notes**

When an adjective or verb stem ends in 르 and is followed by ~어/아, the vowel 으 in 르 is deleted and an additional /ㄹ/ is inserted.

부르 + 어요 → 부르+ㄹ+어요 → 불러요
모르 + 아요 → 모르+ㄹ+아요 → 몰라요
빠르 + 아요 → 빠르+ㄹ+아요 → 빨라요

Dictionary form		~어요/아요	~었/았/ 쓰어요	~어서/아서	~(스)ㅂ니다
(노래) 부르다	to sing, call	불러요	불렀어요	불러서	부릅니다
모르다	to not know	몰라요	몰랐어요	몰라서	모릅니다
빠르다	to be fast	빨라요	빨랐어요	빨라서	빠릅니다

Exercises

1. Use the ~어요/아요 ending in answering the questions.

   (1) 시간이 참 빠르지요? _____

   (2) 마크가 노래를 참 잘 부르지요? _____

   (3) 스티브 씨 일하는 곳 모르지요? _____

   (4) 운동해서 목이 마르지요? _____

2. Conjugate each predicate in parentheses according to its context.

   (1) A: 왜 버스를 안 탔어요?

         B: 택시가 _____ (빠르다) 택시를 탔어요.

   (2) A: 왜 연락 안 했어요?

         B: 전화 번호를 _____ (모르다) 연락 못 했어요.

   (3) A: 어디 가세요?

         B: 노래 _____ (부르다) 노래방에 가요.

   (4) A: 저 분을 잘 아세요?

         B: 아니요, 잘 _____ (모르다).

Narration 민지의 편지

보고 싶은 어머니, 아버지께,

　안녕하셨어요? 할머니께서도 건강하시지요?
그동안 연락 드리지 못해서 정말 죄송합니다. 첫 학기라서
바쁘게 지냈어요. 보내 주신 크리스마스 선물과 편지는 잘
받았습니다. 따뜻한 겨울 옷을 보내 주셔서 정말 고맙습니다.
잘 입을게요.

　그 곳 밴쿠버 날씨는 어때요? 여기 서울 날씨는 요즘 아주
춥습니다. 언니, 오빠 모두 보고 싶습니다. 제 안부 좀 전해
주세요. 그럼 크리스마스 즐겁게 보내세요.
그리고 새해 복 많이 받으세요.

　　　　　　　　　　　　　2020년 12월 19일
　　　　　　　　　　　　　서울에서
　　　　　　　　　　　　　사랑하는 딸 민지 올림

NEW EXPRESSIONS

1. In 연락 드리지 못해서 죄송합니다 'I am very sorry that I was not able to contact you', 연락 means 'contact'. Together with the verb 드리다, it means 'to contact (a superior)' (*lit.* to give contact to a superior). Since the recipients of this letter are Minji's parents, she uses the honorific form 드리다 instead of 주다.

2. The particle 과/와, meaning 'with, and', is more formal than the particles 하고 and (이)랑. 과 is used after a consonant, while 와 follows a vowel as in 책과 가방 and 커피와 차.

3. 안부 (좀) 전해 주세요 is an idiomatic expression meaning 'Please give regards to . . .' This expression can be preceded by [person]한테/께 'to a person'. The particle 께 is used for a senior person whereas 한테 can be used for anybody.

언니한테 안부 (좀) 전해 주세요.	Please give my regards to your sister.
김 선생님께 안부 (좀) 전해 주세요.	Please give my regards to Professor Kim.

4. 크리스마스 즐겁게 보내세요 means 'Merry Christmas'. The Sino-Korean word 성탄절 can be used instead of 크리스마스, as in 성탄절 즐겁게 보내세요.

5. 새해 복 많이 받으세요 means 'Happy New Year' (*lit.* Receive lots of blessings in the new year).

6. 사랑하는 딸 means 'beloved/loving daughter'.

7. 올림 means 'presented by' or 'sincerely yours'. 드림 can be used too.

Exercise

Fill in the blanks with appropriate Korean counterparts.

   (1) Please take good care of your health: _____

   (2) Happy New Year: _____

   (3) Please give my regards to: _____

   (4) Merry Christmas: _____

CULTURE

한국의 종교 (Religions in Korea)

South Korea is a country of great religious diversity and a high degree of religious tolerance. According to a nationwide census done in 2015, about twenty-one million people have an affiliation to a religious tradition, accounting for nearly 43% of the entire population. Christianity and Buddhism are the two biggest religions, making up more than 90% of the religious population. Other minor religious traditions such as Confucianism, Won Buddhism, shamanism, and Islam are active but have only small amounts of followers, according to the census.

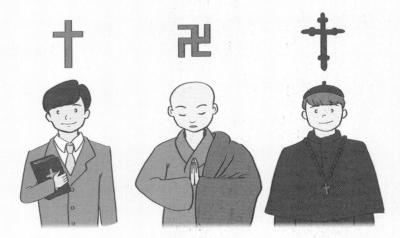

The statistics, however, should be interpreted with caution. First of all, the teachings of Buddhism and Confucianism run deep in the minds of Koreans. This is not surprising considering the long history of Buddhism and Confucianism that began in ancient times. The two religious traditions function more as an ethical code and spiritual guideline than as a religious doctrine for Koreans. Second, traditional shamanism is widely accepted. Like Buddhism and Confucianism, elements of shamanism are often present in Korean life. For example, if you were Korean, you might go see a fortuneteller to ask about when you should get married or when to move to a new place. You might also get a charm from a fortune teller to bring good luck and fend off bad luck. And when you move furniture around in your room, you might take the waterways into consideration according to shamanistic theory.

USAGE

A　Taking a taxi

Translate the following expressions into Korean:

(1)　Please take me to the airport.

_____

(2)　How long will it take to get to the airport?

_____

(3)　Please turn right in front of the bank.

_____

(4)　How much is the fare?

_____

(5)　(Paying the fare) Here is the money. Thank you.

_____

B　Writing letters and postcards

The standard format of a Korean letter to a respected person consists of the following elements:

1.　Salutation:　　_____께 (Dear _____)
2.　Greeting:　　안녕하세요? or 안녕하십니까?
3.　Main text
4.　Closing:　　안녕히 계세요 or 안녕히 계십시오 (계십시오 is a deferential form of 계세요.)
5.　Date: in the order year, month, day ____년 ____월 ____일
6.　Sender's name (followed by 올림/드림 'sincerely' or without it).

▶ **Example**

이민수 선생님께,

선생님 그동안 안녕하셨습니까? 한국어 반 친구들도 다 잘 있습니까?
저는 지난 8월 24일에 서울에 잘 도착했습니다. 요즘 뉴욕의 날씨는
어떻습니까? 여기 서울은 아직 더운 여름 날씨입니다.
저는 학교에서 가까운 곳에 있는 깨끗하고 조용한 아파트로
이사했습니다. 다음 주부터 새 학기가 시작합니다.
거기 한국어 반 친구들한테 안부 전해 주세요.
안녕히 계세요. 다음에 또 연락 드리겠습니다.

2020년 8월 31일
스티브 윌슨 올림

Read Steve's letter and answer the following questions:

(1) 스티브는 언제 서울에 도착했습니까? _____

(2) 서울 날씨는 어떻습니까? _____

(3) 스티브는 언제 이 편지를 썼습니까? _____

(4) 스티브 집은 학교에서 멉니까? _____

(5) 이 편지를 받는 사람은 누구입니까? _____

(6) 언제 새 학기가 시작합니까? _____

(7) 스티브가 사는 아파트는 어떻습니까? _____

In writing addresses on an envelope in Korean, the ordering is from general
to specific: city name, district, street name, house number, the postal code,
then the name of the sender or receiver.

서울특별시 강남구 압구정로 111
김민지

부산광역시 사상구 덕상로 111
박철수

Exercise 1

Imagine that you are writing a first letter to your pen pal, a college student in Korea. Introduce yourself in the letter.

Exercise 2

Imagine that your Korean teacher has gone back to Korea. Write a postcard to him or her in Korean.

Exercise 3

Write a Christmas card in Korean to your classmates.

Exercise 4

Make a Korean version of the following business card.

> **Dongho Lee**, Professor
>
> Dept. of Korean Language
> Korea University
> 111 AnAm-ro, AnAm-dong,
> Seongbuk-gu, Seoul, Korea

Exercise 5

Complete the following letter written by 유미 to her parents.

보고 싶은 부모님께,

안녕하셨어요? 건강하시지요? 그동안 _____ 드리지 못해서 정말 죄송합니다.
첫 학기라서 바쁘게 지냈습니다. 보내 _____ 크리스마스 선물은 잘
받았습니다. _____ 모자를 보내 주셔서 정말 고맙습니다. 잘 _____.
그 곳 시카고 날씨는 어때요? 여기 서울 날씨는 요즘 아주 춥습니다. 할아버지,
할머니도 보고 싶습니다. 제 _____ 좀 전해 주세요. 그럼, 크리스마스
_____ 보내세요. 그리고 새해 _____.

2020년 12월 19일

서울에서

_____ 딸 유미 _____

Lesson 14 On the Telephone

CONVERSATION 1   *It's Saturday, so there's traffic.*

Mark takes a taxi to Incheon International Airport.

Driver:	Where to?
Mark:	Incheon Airport, please. (I noticed) there's a lot of traffic today.
Driver:	That's because it's Saturday.[G14.1]
Mark:	How long will it take to get to the airport? About 30 minutes?
Driver:	Well, we won't be able to get there that fast. I think it will take at least an hour.[G14.2]
Mark:	I see.
	(At the airport)
Driver:	Sir, we're at the airport.
Mark:	How much did it come out to?
Driver:	79,000 Won.
Mark:	Here you go. Thank you.
Driver:	Thank you.

CONVERSATION 2   *I came out to greet somebody.*

Mark runs into Soobin at the airport.

Mark:	Oh Soobin, what brings you here?
Soobin:	Mark, hello! I came out to greet my uncle. What brings you to the airport, Mark?
Mark:	My younger sister is coming from the U.K. today so I came out to greet her.
Soobin:	Ah, really? What time is her flight?
Mark:	It's a 3 o'clock plane but I arrived here a little late.[G14.3]
Soobin:	What did you take to get to the airport?
Mark:	I took a taxi.
Soobin:	The taxi fare must have been a lot. Next time, don't take a taxi.[G14.4]
Mark:	Ah, I didn't know that.[G14.5] I guess I better take the airport bus next time. Where do I catch the airport bus?
Soobin:	There's a stop right in front of the exit.

NARRATION   *Message of Greetings from Minji*

Dear Mom and Dad whom I miss very much,

How are you, is grandmother well, too? I'm really sorry for not being able to write to you all this time. With this being my first semester, I've been pretty busy. I was able to receive the Christmas present and card that you sent. Thank you so much for the warm winter clothes. I'll wear them well.

How is the weather over there in Vancouver? The weather here in Seoul is very cold these days. I miss my older brother and sister too! Please give them my love. Have a merry Christmas and happy New Year!

December 19, 2020
From Seoul
Your beloved daughter, Minji

15과 쇼핑

Lesson 15 Shopping

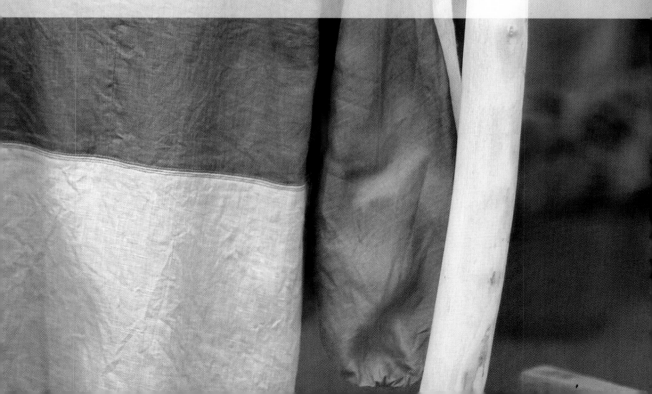

Conversation 1 어서 오세요.

▌ Mark is shopping at Dongdaemun Market.

Conversation 1

점원:	어서 오세요. 뭐 찾으세요?
마크:	까만색 운동화를 찾는데요.
점원:	네, 이쪽으로 와서 보세요.
마크:	저거 얼마예요?
점원:	44,000원이에요.
	사이즈가 어떻게 되세요?
마크:	270인데요. 여기 양말도 팔아요?
점원:	네, 지금 세일이라서 싸게 드릴 수 있어요.^{G15.1}
	세 켤레에 10,000원이에요.
마크:	그럼 운동화하고 양말 세 켤레 주세요.
점원:	네, 금방 갖다 드릴게요.^{G15.2}

NEW WORDS

NOUN

까만색	black (=까망)
사이즈	size
세일	sale
양말	socks, stockings
운동화	sports shoes, sneakers
점원	clerk, salesperson

ADVERB

금방	soon
어서	quick(ly)

COUNTER

번	② number of times (e.g., 한 번, 두 번)
켤레	pair

SUFFIX

~(으)ㄹ 수 있다/없다	can/cannot

VERB

갈아 입다	to change (clothes)
갈아 타다	to change (vehicles)
갖고 가다	to take
갖고 오다	to bring
갖고 다니다	to carry around
갖다 놓다	to bring/put down something somewhere
갖다 주다 / 드리다 *hon.*	to bring/take something to someone
걸어가다	to go on foot
걸어오다	to come on foot
걸어다니다	to walk around
돌아오다	to return, come back
타고 가다	to go riding
타고 오다	to come riding
타고 다니다	to come/go riding

PARTICLE

에	② for, per

NEW EXPRESSIONS

1. 어서 오세요 (*lit.* Come in quickly) is used to welcome customers or guests.

2. 이쪽 means 'this way, this direction'. 쪽 has two meanings: (a) page, e.g., 책 9쪽을 보세요, and (b) direction or side, e.g., 이쪽으로 오세요 'Come this way please', 오른쪽 'the right side', and 왼쪽 'the left side'.

3. The particle 에 in 세 켤레에 means 'for, per'.

4. Shoe size 270 means 270mm.

Exercise

Complete the following dialogue.

점원: _____. 뭐 찾으세요?

손님: _____ 있어요?

점원: 네, 이 쪽으로 오세요.

               여기 많이 있어요.

손님: 이거 _____?

점원: 26,000원입니다.

손님: 저기 저 양말은요?

점원: 한 _____에 2,000원입니다.

Grammar

G15.1   ~(으)ㄹ 수 있다/없다 'possibility / ability'

(1) A: 지금 운전해 **줄 수 있어요**?   Can you drive for me?

      B: 미안해요. 너무 피곤해서 못 해요.

(2) A: 어제 수업에 왜 안 왔어요?

      B: 감기에 걸려서 **갈 수 없었어요**.

(3) A: 전화 좀 **쓸 수 있**을까요?   Can I use your phone?

      B: 그러세요 (=그렇게 하세요).

          전화가 방 안에 있어요.

Examples

✦ Notes

1. The construction [Verb stem~(으)ㄹ 수 있다/없다] 'can/cannot' indicates the possibility or ability of doing something for a given, specific moment.

2. 할 수 없다 is equivalent to 못 하다 and [Verb stem~지 못하다].

> 약속이 있어서 파티에 갈 수 없었어요 (= 가지 못했어요).
> 컴퓨터가 너무 비싸서 살 수 없었어요 (= 사지 못했어요).

Exercises

1. Answer the following questions:

(1) 한국 노래 부를 수 있어요?

<u>네, 부를 수 있어요.</u>

(2) 인터넷에서 운동화도 살 수 있어요?

_____

(3) 한국어 숙제가 어려운데 혼자 할 수 있어요?

_____

(4) 김치를 먹을 수 있어요?

_____

(5) 공항에서 택시를 탈 수 있어요?

_____

2. Interview your partner.

(1) 일하고 싶지요? 무슨 일을 할 수 있어요?

(2) 배가 고프지요? 무슨 음식을 만들 수 있어요?

(3) 밖에 비가 오는데 무슨 운동을 할 수 있어요?

(4) 친구들과 노래방에 가요. 어떤 노래를 부를 수 있어요?

G15.2   Compound verbs

(1)   A: 집에 **걸어 가**세요?   Do you walk home?

    B: 집이 가까워서 학교에   My house is nearby so

          걸어 다녀요.   I walk to school.

(2)   버스가 안 오네요.   The bus is not coming.

    그냥 택시 **타고 갈**까요?   Shall we just take a taxi?

(3)   A: 내일 학교에 사전을 **갖고 갈**까요?

    B: 네, **갖고 오세**요.

Notes

There are many compound verbs in Korean. 가다, 오다, and 다니다 are some commonly used verbs that are used together with other verbs. 가다 adds the meaning of 'to go' and 오다, 'to come', while 다니다 is used for repeated trips.

			가다	오다	다니다
들다	to enter		들어가다	들어오다	-
나다	to exit		나가다	나오다	-
내리다	to descend	~어/아	내려가다	내려오다	-
돌다	to turn		돌아가다	돌아오다	-
오르다	to ascend		올라가다	올라오다	-
걷다	to walk		걸어가다	걸어오다	걸어 다니다

방으로 들어가세요.

한국에서 지난 주에 돌아왔어요.

타다	to ride		타고 가다	타고 오다	타고 다니다
입다	to wear	~고	입고 가다	입고 오다	입고 다니다
갖다	to possess		갖고 가다	갖고 오다	갖고 다니다

학교에 걸어오세요, 차 타고 오세요?

가방에 뭐 갖고 다니세요?

Do you walk to school,
or do you take a car to school?
What do you carry around in
your bag?

			Other verbs
갈다	to change	~어/아	갈아입다 갈아타다

학교에 오는데 버스를 갈아타세요?

옷을 하루에 몇 번 갈아입으세요?

Do you change buses coming
to school?
How many times a day do you
change your clothes?

갖다	to possess	~다(가)	갖다 주다/ 드리다 (humble form)

운동화 좀 갖다 주세요.
할머니께 물 좀 갖다 드리세요.

Bring me the sneakers, please.
Please bring some water for
grandmother.

Exercise

Complete the sentences below with a compound verb from the box. Use appropriate suffixes for each verb.

들어가다	나가다	돌아가다	걸어다니다
갖다 주다	올라가다	갈아타다	갖다 놓다

(1) 엘리베이터를 타고 1층에서 5층까지 [climb and go]

    _____

(2) 여기 물 좀 [get and give] _____

(3) 서점을 찾으세요? 저 쪽 건물에서 왼쪽으로

    [turn and go] _____ 그럼 오른쪽에 있습니다.

(4) 눈이 옵니다. 밖에 [exit and go] _____ 싶어요.

(5) 극장 앞에서 76번 버스로 [change and ride] _____

(6) 차가 없어서 집에서 학교까지 [walk regularly] _____

(7) 날씨가 추워서 방으로 [enter and go] _____

(8) 도서관에서 책을 빌려서 선생님 연구실에 [get and put down]

    _____

✎ Notes

....

....

....

....

....

....

CULTURE

인사동 (Insa-dong)

인사동 is one of the places where visitors to Korea almost always drop by to shop for a souvenir. Located in the center of Seoul, 인사동 is very accessible by public transportation and provides an extensive list of items not readily available anywhere else. From handmade teapots made in the traditional Korean style to silken 한복 with dashing colors and patterns, 인사동 symbolizes traditional Korea as it is known to the world.

Aside from being a center for souvenir shopping, 인사동 is also well known for its many art galleries. In between visits to souvenir shops, you can walk into the art galleries scattered about the area and appreciate both traditional and modern Korean art. If you get thirsty, you can go to cafés that serve traditional teas, Korean-style shaved ice, and other tasty treats. 인사동 is a popular place even for Korean people to have Korean food. You might also find it interesting that some franchise stores in 인사동 even have their storefront signs written in Korean.

Adjacent to 인사동 are 종로 and 삼청동, which are popular for their cafés, restaurants, boutiques, and art galleries. 경복궁 is at the entrance to 인사동, and other Joseon dynasty palaces such as 창덕궁, 창경궁, and 덕수궁 are only a couple of blocks away. 서울시청, 종묘, 광화문 광장, and 청계천 are other attractions close to 인사동.

Conversation 2　　이 서점에 자주 오세요?

▐ Soobin and Woojin meet at Kyobo Bookstore.

Conversation 2

수빈:　아, 우진 씨. 책 사러 오셨어요?

우진:　네, 친구 졸업 선물을 사러 왔어요.

수빈:　이 서점에는 자주 오세요?

우진:　네, 거리도 제일 가깝고 늦게까지 문을 열어서
　　　　자주 와요. 수빈 씨는요?

수빈:　저도 가끔 와서 커피 마시면서^{G15.3}
　　　　잡지도 보고 그래요. 오늘은 별로 할 일이^{G15.4}
　　　　없어서 그냥 책 좀 보러 왔어요.

우진:　그래요? 그럼 친구 선물을 아직 못 골랐는데
　　　　커피 마시고 나서^{G15.5} 저 좀 도와 줄래요?

수빈:　네, 그럼요.

NEW WORDS

NOUN

거리	① distance; ② street
계획(하다)	plan
등산(하다)	hiking
목욕(하다)	bath
문	door
샤워(하다)	shower
잡지	magazine
졸업(하다)	graduation
화장실	bathroom, restroom

ADVERB

별로	not really
제일	first, most

VERB

구경하다	to look around; to sightsee
고르다	to choose, select
세수하다	to wash one's face
손(을) 씻다	to wash one's hands
열다	to open
이(를) 닦다	to brush one's teeth

SUFFIX

~고 나서	after
~(으)면서	while ~ing
~(으)ㄹ	noun-modifying form (prospective)

NEW EXPRESSIONS

1. Here are some useful words and expressions indicating frequency:

가끔	once in a while
자주	often
한 번도 안	not even once, never
얼마나 자주	how often?
매일 (=날마다)	every day
하루에 한 번	once a day
하루에 한 번쯤	about once a day
한 달에 두 번	twice a month
일주일에 한 번쯤	about once a week
일 년에 두 번쯤	about twice a year

2. [N도 V~고 그래요] is used when enumerating several possibilities. The particle 도 is added to a noun(s), and the suffix ~고 is attached to the verb stem(s).

3. 별로 usually occurs with a negative verb or adjective. It means 'not particularly, not really, not so much'.

Exercise

Complete the following sentences using the words in the box below.

가끔   별로   자주   보통   이젠   매일

(1) 집에 얼마나 _____ 전화하세요?

(2) 나는 _____ 수영을 안 해요.

(3) 그 영화는 _____ 재미없어요.

(4) 나는 _____ 아침 운동을 해요.

(5) 나는 _____ 한국 영화를 봐요.

(6) 내 룸메이트는 _____ 아침을 안 먹어요.

Grammar

G15.3   ~(으)면서 'while ~ing'

(1) 내 친구는 등산하**면서** 보통 음악을 들어요.

(2) 운전하**면서** 전화하지 마세요.   Do not make phone calls
                                             while driving.

(3) 저는 보통 아침을 먹**으면서** 신문을 읽어요.

(4) 폴은 샤워하**면서** 이를 닦았어요.

Examples

Notes

1. ~(으)면서 'while' is used to express two simultaneous actions carried out by the same subject.

2. Note that tense is not marked in the subordinate clause, but is determined by the main clause as in (4).

Exercises

1. What else can you do while you are engaged in the following activity?

    (1) 음악을 듣다   <u>음악을 들으면서 책을 읽어요</u>.

    (2) 커피를 마시다 _____

    (3) 운전하다   _____

    (4) 신문을 읽다   _____

    (5) 아침을 먹다   _____

    (6) 걸어가다   _____

2. Ask your partner these questions, and tell the class the answers.

    (1) 빨래를 하면서 보통 뭐 해요?   _____

    (2) 아침을 먹으면서 신문을 읽어요?   _____

    (3) 라디오를 들으면서 공부해요?   _____

    (4) 영화 보면서 보통 뭐 먹어요?   _____

    (5) 버스를 기다리면서 보통 뭐 해요?   _____

G15.4   The noun-modifying form [Verb~(으)ㄹ] + N (prospective)

    (1) A: 이번 주말에 **할** 일이 많아요?   Do you have lots of things to do this weekend?

           B: 네, 좀 많아요.   Yes, I do.

    (2) 생일 파티에 **입을** 옷이 없어요.   I don't have clothes to wear to the birthday party.

    (3) 다음 학기에 한국어를 **가르치실** 분은 박 선생님이세요.   The person who will teach Korean next semester is Professor Park.

Examples

◆   Notes

The noun-modifying form ~(으)ㄹ indicates that a situation is yet to be realized. In (1) above, 할 일 means 'things to do', in (2) 입을 옷 'clothes to wear', and in (3) 가르치실 분 'the person who will teach'.

Exercises

1. Fill in the blanks with the ~(으)ㄹ form.

    (1) 오늘 저녁에 (먹다)_____ 음식이 없어요.

    (2) 내년 여름에 한국에 (가다)_____ 친구들이 많이 있어요.

    (3) 다음 학기에 (졸업하다)_____ 학생이 두 사람 있어요.

    (4) 목이 말라요. (마시다)_____ 물 좀 주세요.

2. Translate the following sentences into Korean using the ~(으)ㄹ form:

    (1) This is the present that I will give to my older brother.

    (2) Professor Kim is the teacher who will teach us from next week on.

    (3) This is the newspaper that I will read in the lounge.

    (4) There are lots of things to do this weekend.

G15.5   The clausal connective ~고 나서

(1)	A:	언제 숙제 했어요?	When did you do your homework?	
	B:	목욕 **하고 나서** 했어요.	I did it after taking a shower.	
(2)	A:	수업 끝나**고 나서** 뭐 할 거예요?		
	B:	백화점에 신발 구경하러 갈 거예요.		
(3)	A:	졸업하**고 나서** 뭐 하고 싶어요?		
	B:	아직 계획 못 했어요.		

Examples

◆ Notes

The construction [Verb stem~고 나서] is used when one event or activity has just been finished and another is forthcoming. The event in the main clause occurs after the first action is finished. The ~고 나서 form is attached only to a verb stem, not to an adjective stem. It is more definitive than [Verb stem~고] because the first action is actually finished before the second starts. Note that the past tense is not used in the first clause.

Exercises

1. Describe the actions shown in the illustrations in sequence.

(1)–(2)   공부하고 나서 점심 먹었어요.

(2)–(3)   점심 먹고 나서 _____

(3)–(4)   _____

(4)–(5)   _____

(5)–(6)   _____

(1)   (2)   (3)

(4)   (5)   (6)

2. Using ~고 나서, fill in the blanks according to the context.

(1) 스티브는 6시에 저녁을 먹습니다. <u>저녁을 먹고 나서</u> 도서관에 가서 공부를 합니다. <u>도서관에서 공부하고 나서</u> 집에 10시에 옵니다.

(2) 우진은 9시에 한국어 수업이 있습니다. _____ 10시에 랩에 가서 한국어 연습을 합니다. _____ 11시 반에 학교 식당에서 친구를 만납니다.

(3) 친구를 만나서 12시에 점심을 먹습니다. _____ 1시에 테니스를 칩니다. _____ 3시에 도서관에 가서 공부를 합니다. _____ 6시쯤 기숙사에 돌아옵니다. 기숙사에 돌아와서 6시 반쯤 저녁을 먹습니다.

(4) 아침에 일어나서 화장실에 가서 손을 씻습니다. _____ 이를 닦습니다. _____ 세수합니다.

3. Fill in the blanks with ~고 나서 and an event that can serve as a time reference.

(1) A: 내일 백화점에 몇 시쯤 가실래요?
     B: 수업 <u>끝나고 나서</u> 1시쯤 어때요?
     A: 네, 좋아요.

(2) A: 저녁에 보통 뭐 해요?
     B: _____

(3) A: 숙제 때문에 뵙고 싶은데 몇 시쯤 갈까요?
     B: _____ 10시쯤 어때요?
     A: 네, 괜찮습니다.
         그럼 수업 끝나고 10시에 뵙겠습니다.

(4) A: 한국어 숙제 언제 했어요?
     B: _____

Narration 　　　동대문 시장

어젯밤에 지하철을 타고 동대문 시장¹에 갔습니다.
동대문 시장은 옷과 신발 등²을 파는 한국에서 제일 큰
시장입니다. 물건³이 아주 많고 가격⁴도 쌉니다. 그래서
많은 사람들이 동대문 시장에 쇼핑을 하러 갑니다. 그리고
동대문 시장은 24시간 문을 열어서 구경하러 걸어다니는
사람들이 많습니다. 시장에서 물건도 사고 옷과 신발도
구경하고 맛있는 음식을 사 먹기(=사서 먹기)도 합니다.
저는 까만색 운동화와 양말도 사고 김밥⁵도 사 먹었습니다.
운동화와 양말은 세일이라서 아주 쌌습니다. 김밥도 아주
맛있었습니다. 옷 가게와 신발 가게들이 많아서 구경할 게
정말 많았습니다. 다음 주말에도 셔츠와 바지를 사러 또 가고
싶습니다.

1. 동대문 시장: Dongdaemun Market　　2. 등: etc.
3. 물건: merchandise　　　　　　　　4. 가격: price　　　　5. 김밥: *gimbap*

Exercises

1. List the things you can buy at 동대문 시장.

2. Fill in the blanks based on the narration.

   (1) 동대문 시장은 한국에서 _____ 큰 시장입니다.

   (2) 동대문 시장에서는 _____과 _____ 등을 팝니다.

   (3) 동대문 시장은 _____ 문을 엽니다.

   (4) 동대문 시장에서 사람들은 _____ 을 구경하고
       맛있는 _____을 사 먹기도 합니다.

✏️ Notes

....

....

....

....

....

....

USAGE

A *Asking about prices; buying things*

얼마예요 is used to ask about prices or fares.

A:	이거 얼마예요?	How much is this?
B:	[price] + 원(₩)/불($)이에요.	It is _____ ₩/$.

Exercise 1

Prepare some shopping lists and exchange the following question and answer.

Example:

$185   A: 시계 얼마예요?

B: 백팔십오 불이에요.

Exercise 2

Play the roles of customer and salesperson.

A: 이 연필 얼마예요?

B: 일 불 오십 전(cent)이에요.

(1) $1.50

(2) $0.32

(3) $15.60

(4) $7.20

(5) $19.90

(6) $8.00

Exercise 3

Practice the following dialogue.

> A: 이거 어디서 샀어요?
>
> B: '하나 백화점'에서 샀어요.
>
> A: 얼마 줬어요?   'How much did you pay?'
>
> B: _____원/불 줬어요.

Using the model dialogue above, ask about things that belong to your classmates.

B   *Expressing frequency*

얼마나 자주 . . . 어요/아요? means 'How often do you . . . ?' See how it is used in the exchange below.

> A: 부모님께 얼마나 자주 연락하세요?
>
> B: 일주일에 한 번쯤 전화해요.

Exercise 1

Talk with your partner about how often each person at the table engages in each activity.

> A: 스티브는 얼마나 자주 쇼핑해요?
>
> B: 한 달에 한 번 쇼핑해요.

Name	Shopping	Dating	Coming to school	Exercising	Writing letters
스티브	once a month	once a month	MTWTh (4 times a week)	every day	once a year
민지	every week	once a week	every day	once a month	twice a year
마크	twice a month	never	MWF	twice a week	once a week

Exercise 2

Interview your classmates.

(1) 백화점에 쇼핑하러 얼마나 자주 가세요?

(2) 얼마나 자주 머리를 자르세요? (머리를 자르다 'to get a haircut')

(3) 얼마나 자주 외식하세요? (외식하다 'to eat out')

(4) 얼마나 자주 영화 보러 영화관에 가세요?

(5) 얼마나 자주 정장을 입으세요? (정장 'formal suit or dress')

Exercise 3

Answer the following questions in Korean:

(1) 올림픽은 얼마나 자주 있어요? (올림픽 'Olympic')

(2) 미국의 대통령 선거는 몇 년에 한 번 있어요? (대통령 선거 'presidential election')

(3) 월드컵은 얼마나 자주 해요? (월드컵 'World Cup')

(4) 학교 신문은 얼마나 자주 나와요?

(5) 한국어 시험은 얼마나 자주 봐요?

Notes

Lesson 15 Shopping

CONVERSATION 1	*Welcome.*

Mark is shopping at Dongdaemun Marketplace.

Sales Clerk:	Welcome. Are you looking for anything in particular?
Mark:	I'm looking for black sneakers.
Sales Clerk:	Ah yes, right this way please.
Mark:	How much is that?
Sales Clerk:	44,000 Won. What size are you?
Mark:	270 mm . . . do you sell socks too?
Sales Clerk:	Yes, they're on sale now, so I can give them to you at an inexpensive price.[G15.1] It's 10,000 Won for three pairs.
Mark:	Then give me three pairs of socks with the sneakers, please.
Store Clerk:	Yes, I'll get those for you right away.[G15.2]

CONVERSATION 2	*Do you come to this bookstore often?*

Soobin and Woojin meet at Kyobo Bookstore.

Soobin:	Oh, Woojin! Did you come to buy a book?
Woojin:	Yes, I came to buy my friend's graduation present.
Soobin:	Do you come to this bookstore often?
Woojin:	Yes, it's the closest one and stays open until late so I come here often. What about you?
Soobin:	I also sometimes come here and read some magazines while I drink coffee.[G15.3] Today, I didn't have anything in particular to do,[G15.4] so I just came to look at some books.
Woojin:	Really? Well, I still haven't been able to pick a present for my friend; would you care to help me out after you finish your coffee?[G15.5]
Soobin:	Sure, of course.

NARRATION · *Dongdaemun Marketplace*

Last night I took the subway and went to Dongdaemun Marketplace. Dong-daemun Marketplace is the biggest marketplace in Korea that sells various things like clothes, shoes, etc. There is an abundance of things to buy and the prices are cheap too, so a lot of people go to shop at Dongdaemun Market-place. Also, Dongdaemun Marketplace is open twenty-four hours a day so there are a lot of people who walk to look around. They buy things from the shops, look around at clothes and shoes, and even buy and eat tasty food. I bought black sneakers, socks, and even *gimbap*. As for the sneakers and socks, they were on sale so they were very cheap. The *gimbap* was very delicious too. There are many clothing and shoe stores so there really are a lot of things to see. I want to go again next weekend too, to buy some shirts and pants.

16과 음식점에서

Lesson 16 At a Restaurant

Conversation 1   냉면 먹어 봤어요?

Conversation   1

Soobin, Soobin's mom, Woojin, and Mark enter a Korean restaurant.
At the restaurant:

종업원: 어서 오세요. 몇 분이세요?

우진: 네 명인데요. 자리 있어요?

종업원: 네, 이쪽으로 오세요.

Everybody sits at the table. The server brings water and menus.

종업원: 주문하시겠어요?

수빈 어머니: 저는 비빔밥 주세요.

우진: 저는 순두부찌개 먹을게요.

수빈: 전 불고기하고 냉면 먹을래요.

                마크 씨, 냉면 먹어 봤어요?G16.1

마크: 네, 학교 식당에서 한 번 먹어 봤는데

                괜찮았어요. 그런데 저는 찬 음식을

                별로 안 좋아하기 때문에G16.2 육개장 먹을래요.

종업원: 네, 알겠습니다. 금방 갖다 드리겠습니다.

NEW WORDS

NOUN

과자	chips, cookies, crackers
냉면	*naengmyeon* (cold buckwheat noodles)
라면	instant noodles (ramen)
밥	① cooked rice; ② meal
볼링	bowling
비빔밥	*bibimbap* (rice with vegetables and beef)
순두부찌개	soft tofu stew
육개장	spicy beef soup
음식점	restaurant (=식당)
자리	seat
종업원	employee
케이크	cake

VERB

물어보다	to inquire
싫어하다	to dislike
주문하다	to order

ADJECTIVE

뜨겁다	to be hot
시원하다	to be cool, refreshing
싫다	to be undesirable
차다	to be cold

SUFFIX

~기	nominalizer
~기 때문에	because
~어/아 보다	to try doing

NEW EXPRESSIONS

1. In 이쪽, 그쪽, and 저쪽, 쪽 indicates direction. 으로 'to, toward' is attached to 쪽, as in 이쪽으로, 그쪽으로, and 저쪽으로, which are synonymous with 이리(로), 그리(로), and 저리(로).

2. Both 주문하다 and 시키다 mean 'to order'. While 주문하다 can refer to any kind of ordering, 시키다 is restricted to ordering in a restaurant.

Exercises

1. Fill in the blanks with appropriate words.

    (1) 음식을 사서 먹는 곳: <u>식당</u>

    (2) 식당에서 주문을 받는 사람: _____

    (3) 식당에서 주문을 하는 사람: _____

    (4) 식당 테이블('table')과 의자: _____

2. List the names of the Korean foods you know.

Grammar

G16.1   ~어/아 보다 'try doing'

Examples

(1) A: 비빔밥 **먹어 봤**어요?   Have you eaten *bibimbap*?

   B: 아니요, 안 **먹어 봤**어요.   No, I have not.

(2) A: 이 과자 한번 **드셔 보**세요.   Please try this cracker.

   B: 감사합니다. 아주 맛있어요.   Thank you. It is very

                                delicious.

(3) A: 밖에 친구가 왔어요.   (My) friend is outside.

        나가 보세요.   Please (*lit.* try) go out and see

                                him.

Notes

1. The first example above literally means 'Did you eat *bibimbap* and see what it was like?' It is different from 비빔밥 먹었어요? 'Did you eat *bibimbap*?' which is a factual question. When ~어/아 보다 is used, it indicates an experience ('have done') or an attempt ('try') as shown below.

   한국에 한번 **가 보**세요.   Please try going to Korea.

2. With the meaning of 'attempt' or 'trial', ~어/아 보다 can be used to express suggestion in the form of ~어/아 보세요.

   이 책 재미있어요. 읽어 보세요.
   오후에 텔레비전 보지 말고 운동해 보세요.
   다음에는 한국 노래를 들어 보세요.

3. Adding 보다 to a verb sometimes creates a new compound verb. For example, 알다 + 보다 = 알아보다 'to inquire into, recognize', and 묻다 + 보다 = 물어보다 'to inquire, ask'.

A: 학교 전화 번호를 모르는데 누구한테 물어보지요?

B: 114*에 전화해서 알아보세요.

(*In Korea, people dial 114 for directory assistance)

There is an idiomatic expression 그만 가 보겠습니다 'Let me excuse myself' (*lit.* With that much, I will try leaving). In this expression, 보다(보겠습니다) adds a nuance of politeness.

Exercises

1. Answer the following questions.

   (1) 도서관에서 일해 봤어요?   _____

   (2) 정치학 수업을 들어 봤어요?   _____

   (3) 라면 먹어 봤어요?   _____

   (4) 서울에 가 봤어요?   _____

   (5) 테니스 쳐 봤어요?   _____

2. Ask your partner whether he or she has had the following experiences, and then switch roles.

   (1) 볼링 치다   Q: 볼링 쳐 봤어요?

                            A: 작년에 한 번 쳐 봤어요.

   (2) 호주를 여행하다

   (3) 한국 신문을 읽다

   (4) 뉴욕에서 택시를 타다

   (5) 한국 음식점에 가다

   (6) 갈비를 먹다

3. Suggest the following food to your partner:

(1) 육개장   A: 육개장 <u>드셔 보세요</u>.
                      B: 네, 감사합니다.

(2) 따뜻한 커피 한 잔

(3) 시원한 냉면

(4) 뜨거운 라면

(5) 생일 케이크

G16.2   The clausal connective ~기 때문에 (reason)

Examples

(1) 돈이 없**기 때문에** 책을 못 사요.   Because I don't have
                                            money, I can't buy books.

(2) 이번 주는 시험이 있**기 때문에**
     일을 못 해요.

(3) 한국어 수업 시간에 말하**기**,   In Korean class, we learn
     듣**기**, 읽**기**, 쓰**기**를 배웁니다.   speaking, listening, reading,
                                            and writing.

(4) A: 방학이 벌써 끝났네요.
     B: 공부하**기** 싫어요. 더 놀고 싶어요.

Notes

1. ~기 때문에 'Because . . .' gives a reason, unlike ~어서/아서 (G10.4), which refers to a cause or a sequence. While 때문에 is preceded by a noun (G13.4), the nominalizer ~기 in ~기 때문에 is used with a verb or an adjective.

수업 때문에 = 수업이 있기 때문에

2. ~기 때문에 differs from ~어서/아서 in some respects:

(a) ~기 때문에 is used with a tense marker, while ~어서/아서 cannot take any tense marker.

머리가 아파서 타이레놀을 먹었어요.
머리가 아팠기 때문에 타이레놀을 먹었어요.

(b) When you make an excuse, an apology, or an expression of gratitude, it is more appropriate to use ~어서/아서, which implies a situation beyond your control and thus inevitable.

늦어서 미안합니다.　　(Not 늦었기 때문에 미안합니다.)
와 주셔서 감사합니다.　(Not 와 주셨기 때문에 감사합니다.)

3. The nominalizer ~기 is used to form a noun out of a verb, as in the English gerund ~ing as in (3). Sometimes ~는 것 and ~기 are used interchangeably, as in:

수업 시간에 쓰**기**를 배워요.　　(We) learn writing in class.
수업 시간에 쓰**는 것**을 배워요.　(We) learn how to write in class.

Exercises

1. Change the first clause using ~기 때문에. Use the past-tense form if necessary.

(1)　수지는 아침을 (안 먹다) ＿＿＿＿＿＿＿＿＿ 점심을 일찍 먹어요.

(2)　저는 매일 (운동하다) ＿＿＿＿＿＿＿＿＿ 건강합니다.

(3)　민지가 점심을 (사다) ＿＿＿＿＿＿＿＿＿ 우진이가 커피를 샀습니다.

(4)　토요일 오후에는 교통이 (복잡하다) ＿＿＿＿＿＿＿＿＿
　　　지하철을 타요.

(5)　찬 음식을 (싫어하다) ＿＿＿＿＿＿＿＿＿ 냉면을 자주 먹지 않아요.

2. Give a reason in response to the following questions using ~기 때문에.

    (1) A: 왜 피곤해요?

          B: _____

    (2) A: 왜 육개장을 안 먹어요?

          B: _____

    (3) A: 왜 어제 산 텔레비전을 다시 가게에 갖다 주었어요?

          B: _____

    (4) A: 왜 한국어를 배우고 있어요?

          B: _____

    (5) A: 오늘 왜 수업에 늦었어요?

          B: _____

3. Ask your partner the following questions. Answers should include ~기 때문에, ~어요/아요, ~(으)ㄹ 거예요, or ~어야/아야 돼요.

    (1) A: 학교에 몇 시에 가세요?

          B: 한국어 수업이 있기 때문에 9시까지 가야 돼요.

    (2) A: 주말에 어디 갈 거예요?

          B: _____

    (3) A: 이번 방학에 뭐 할 거예요?

          B: _____

    (4) A: 오늘 몇 시에 점심 먹을 거예요?

          B: _____

    (5) A: 오늘 도서관에서 공부할 거예요?

          B: _____

    (6) A: 오늘 저녁 어디서 먹을 거예요?

          B: _____

4. Use ~기 to describe what each person below enjoys doing.

(1) 마이클은 주말에 등산을 **해요**.

마이클은 주말에 등산**하기를** 좋아해요.

(2) 제니는 영화를 봐요.

_____

(3) 리사는 예쁜 선물을 받아요.

_____

(4) 우진은 방학에 여행을 가요.

_____

(5) 수빈은 어머니하고 전화해요.

_____

(6) 스티브는 음악을 들어요.

_____

✏️ **Notes**

_____

· ·

· ·

· ·

· ·

· ·

· ·

Conversation 2   육개장이 맵지 않아요?

Conversation   2

■ The server brings food.

종업원: 여기 음식 나왔습니다.
            비빔밥 어느 분이세요?

수빈: 어머니 앞에 놓아 주세요.

종업원: 냉면 잘라 드릴까요?^{G16.4}

수빈: 네, 잘라 주세요.

마크, 우진: 잘 먹겠습니다, 어머님.

수빈 어머니: 육개장이 너무 맵지 않아요?^{G16.5}

마크: 괜찮습니다. 아주 맛있어요.
            우진 씨, 순두부찌개는 어때요?

우진: 별로 짜지 않고 맛있어요.

수빈 어머니: (종업원에게) 저 . . . 여기요!
            김치하고 반찬 좀 더 주세요.

종업원: 네.

■ After a while

마크, 우진: 정말 잘 먹었습니다.

수빈 어머니: 여기요! 계산서 좀 갖다 주시겠어요?

종업원: 네, 알겠습니다.

NEW WORDS

NOUN

값	price
계산서	check
김치	*kimchi*
녹차	green tea
된장찌개	soybean-paste stew
메뉴	menu
반찬	side dish
샌드위치	sandwich
식사(하다)	meal
음료수	beverage
중(에서)	among, between
피자	pizza

VERB

놓아 주다/드리다 *hum.*	to put something down (for someone)
돌려 주다/드리다 *hum.*	to return (something to someone)
시키다	to order (food)
잘라 주다/드리다 *hum.*	to cut (something for someone)

ADJECTIVE

달다	to be sweet
맵다	to be spicy
않다	to not be, to not do
짜다	to be salty

SUFFIX

~어/아 드리다 *hum.*	do something for another's benefit

NEW EXPRESSIONS

1. Flavors and tastes:

맛	flavor, taste	맛이 있다	to be tasty
		맛이 없다	to not taste good
달다	to taste sweet	쓰다	to taste bitter
싱겁다	to taste bland	짜다	to taste salty
맵다	to taste spicy	시다	to taste sour

2. People also attract a server's attention by calling out 여기요! (*lit.* Over here!).

3. 잘 먹겠습니다 or 맛있게 먹겠습니다 is used as a polite acknowledgment before eating to thank the host, and 잘 먹었습니다 or 맛있게 먹었습니다 after you eat.

4. Parents of your friends are often addressed as 아버님 (honorific form of 아버지) and 어머님 (honorific form of 어머니) as in 잘 먹겠습니다, 어머님.

Exercises

1. Practice ordering food at a Korean restaurant.

메뉴

갈비	₩29,000
불고기	₩23,000
비빔밥	₩ 8,500
냉면	₩ 9,000
육개장	₩ 8,000
순두부찌개	₩ 7,500

종업원:　　어서 오세요. 몇 분이세요?

손님:　　　_____. 자리가 있어요?

종업원:　　네, 이쪽으로 오세요.

　　　　　　주문하시겠어요?

손님:　　　_____하고 _____ 주세요.

(after a while)

손님:　　　여기요! _____ 더 주세요.

종업원:　　네, 알겠습니다.

2. Ask your classmates what foods they like and dislike.

이름	좋아하는 음식	싫어하는 음식

G16.3 Giving and offering: ~어/아 드리다

(1) 어머니가 뜨거운 음식을 싫어하세요.
그래서 냉면을 **시켜 드렸**어요.　　I ordered *naengmyeon* for my mom.

(2) A: 할아버지 생신에 뭘 **해 드렸**어요?　What did you do for your grandfather on his birthday?

B: 식당에서 저녁을 **사 드렸**어요.　I bought him dinner at a restaurant.

(3) A: 책 좀 **빌려 주**세요.　　Please lend me a book.

B: 네, **빌려 드릴**게요.　　Sure, I'll lend it to you.

A: 언제까지 **돌려 드릴**까요?　By when should I return it to you?

B: 모레까지 **돌려 주**세요.　Please return it by the day after tomorrow.

  Notes

1. The difference between 주다 and 드리다 is illustrated in the picture below. The plain form 주다 is used to a person of lower status whereas its humble form 드리다 is used to a senior person or one of higher status (G9.3).

　　아버지께서 저한테 가방을 사 주셨어요.

　　제가 아버지께 가방을 사 드렸어요.

　　소피아가 저한테 가방을 사 주었어요.

2. The different forms of ~어/아 주다 are as follows:

~어/아 주다 Plain	유진이가 커피를 사 주었습니다.
~어/아 주시다 Subject honorific	선생님께서 저한테 점심을 사 주셨습니다.
~어/아 드리다 Subject humble (recipient honorific)	나는 어머니께 꽃을 사 드렸습니다.
~어/아 드리시다 Subject honorific and humble	어머니께서 할머니께 옷을 사 드리셨습니다.

Exercises

1. Complete the dialogues, using the proper forms of 주다 or 드리다.

   (1) 종업원: 음료수는 뭐 드릴까요?

        손님: 녹차 _____

   (2) 학생: 뭐 시켜 드릴까요?

        선생님: 된장찌개를 _____

   (3) 선생님: 어제 할머니께 책을 읽어 드렸어요?

        학생: 네, 읽어 _____

2. Complete the sentences with one of the verbs of giving in the box below. Use an appropriate suffix for each verb.

주다   주시다   드리다   드리시다

   (1) 어머니가 저한테 돈을 _____

   (2) 내가 친구한테 샌드위치를 만들어 _____

   (3) 저기요, 할머니께 물 좀 갖다 _____

   (4) 선생님께서 아버지께 편지를 보내 _____

3. Answer the following questions using ~어/아 주다.

    (1)   계산서 드릴까요?

          네, _____

    (2)   볼펜 좀 빌려 주시겠어요?

          _____

    (3)   냉면은 나중에 시킬까요?

          _____

    (4)   메뉴 갖다 드릴까요?

          _____

Notes

G16.4   Negation: ~지 않다

Statements:

(1)   a. 날씨가 **안** 좋아요.   The weather is not good (at all).
      b. 날씨가 좋**지 않**아요.   The weather is not good.

(2)   작년에는 한국말을 배우**지 않**았습니다.
      시간이 별로 없어서 한국어 수업을 듣**지 않**습니다.

Questions:

(3)   A: 주스가 너무 달**지 않**아요?   Isn't the juice too sweet?
      B: 네, 좀 달아요.

(4)   A: 어젯밤에 극장에 사람이
            많**지 않**았어요?
      B: 네, 정말 많았어요.

Examples

Notes

1. In general, the long form of the negative ~지 않다 and the short form [안 + Verb or Adjective] are used interchangeably, although the long form sounds slightly more formal. The long form is much more frequently used in writing than is the short form.

2. ~지 못하다 'cannot' (G14.2) is used instead of ~지 않다 when a situation or external circumstances do not allow a person to do something as in (2).

3. The long form of the negative is used in conversation when the speaker seeks confirmation or agreement from the listener. Stating a belief or an opinion as a negative question is more cautious and more polite as in (3) and (4).

Exercises

Exercises

1. Change the following sentences by using the form ~지 않다.

    (1) 오늘은 별로 안 바빠요.

        <u>오늘은 별로 바쁘지 않아요.</u>

    (2) 종업원이 계산서를 빨리 안 갖다 줬어요.

        _____

    (3) 내일 백화점에 같이 안 갈래요?

        _____

    (4) 오늘은 피자를 안 먹고 싶어요.

        _____

    (5) 친구가 돈을 안 빌려 줬어요.

        _____

    (6) 이 식당은 음식 값이 별로 안 싸요.

        _____

2. Give an appropriate response using the form ~지 않아요?

    (1) 밖이 춥습니다. 룸메이트가 짧은 바지를 입고 나갑니다.

        <u>춥지 않아요?</u>

    (2) 더운 여름날 아버지가 뜨거운 차를 드십니다.

        _____

    (3) 스티브 씨가 매운 김치를 먹습니다.

        _____

    (4) 아직 식사를 못 했습니다.

        _____

    (5) 언니가 밤에 안 자고 공부합니다.

        _____

G16.5 The comparative 보다 (더) 'more than'

(1) A: 갈비가 냉면**보다** 비싸지요? — *Galbi* is more expensive than *naengmyeon*, isn't it?

B: 그럼요. 갈비가 **더** 비싸요. — Yes, *galbi* is more expensive.

(2) A: 백화점에 버스를 타고 갈까요?

B: 버스**보다** 지하철이 **더** 빨라요.

(3) A: 순두부찌개와 된장찌개 **중에서** 어느 것을 더 좋아하세요?

B: 저는 된장찌개를 **더** 좋아해요.

(4) A: 미국 어디에 한국 사람들이 **제일** 많아요? — Where in the United States has the greatest number of Koreans?

B: 로스앤젤레스하고 뉴욕에 **제일** 많이 살아요.

Notes

1. The comparative construction in Korean employs the particle 보다 '(rather) than' and the adverbs 더 'more' and 덜 'less'. Like all other particles, 보다 follows the noun being compared (e.g., 책보다 '[rather] than a book', 불고기보다 '[rather] than *bulgogi*'). Word order between the two nouns being compared is free, and the adverb 더 can be omitted as shown in (1A). 중에서 'between, among' can also be used as needed as shown in (3).

B보다 A가 더 / A가 B보다 더		'A is more than B'
냉면보다 갈비가 더 비싸요.	=	갈비가 냉면보다 더 비싸요.
B 보다 A가 덜 / A가 B보다 덜		'A is less than B'
갈비보다 냉면이 덜 비싸요.	=	냉면이 갈비보다 덜 비싸요.

2. Comparison in questions has the following word order: nouns being compared + question word + adjective.

이 두 사람 중에서 누가 더 커요?	Between these two people, who is taller?
한국어와 영어 중에서 어느 것이 더 어려워요?	Between Korean and English which is more difficult?
테니스하고 골프 중에서 어느 것이 더 쉬워요?	Between tennis and golf, which is easier?

3. Superlative constructions use 제일 or, in writing, 가장.

이 책이 제일 비싸요.	This book is the most expensive.
제일 노래 잘 하는 가수는 누구예요?	Who is the best singer?
미국에서 가장 살고 싶은 도시는 어디입니까?	Which American city do you want to live in the most?

Exercises

1. Compare the following items:

(1) 한국어, 영어 : _____

(2) 지하철, 버스 : _____

(3) 뉴욕, 밴쿠버 : _____

(4) 미국, 호주 : _____

(5) 의사, 교수 : _____

(6) 커피, 녹차: _____

(7) 여름, 겨울 : _____

(8) 여자, 남자 : _____

2. Compare the prices and say which one is more expensive and by how much.

(1)   불고기 $24   갈비 $29

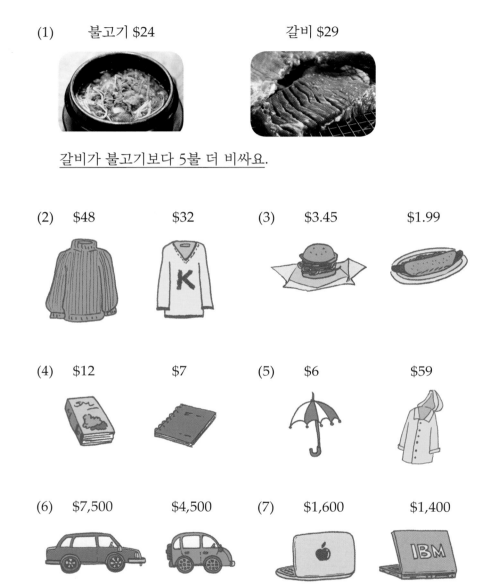

갈비가 불고기보다 5불 더 비싸요.

(2) $48 $32   (3) $3.45 $1.99

(4) $12 $7   (5) $6 $59

(6) $7,500 $4,500   (7) $1,600 $1,400

3. Answer the following questions:

  (1) 백화점보다 물건이 더 싼 곳은 어디예요?

  (2) 한국어보다 더 쉬운 과목은 어느 것이에요?

  (3) 스타워즈보다 더 재미있는 영화는 뭐예요?

  (4) 불고기와 갈비 중에서 어느 것이 더 맛있어요?

  (5) 한국어와 중국어 중에서 어느 것이 더 배우기 어려울까요?

4. Ask your partner the following questions:

  (1) 제일 좋아하는 음식이 뭐에요?

  (2) 음료수 중에서 뭐를 제일 좋아해요?

  (3) 학교 근처 식당 중에서 어디가 제일 서비스가 좋아요?

  (4) 제일 잘 만들 수 있는 음식이 뭐에요?

✎ **Notes**

| Narration | 점심 식사 |

오늘 우진이[1]와 민지는 학교 앞 '우리식당'에서 점심을
먹었습니다. 학교 앞에는 음식점들이 여러 군데 있는데,
값도 싸고 종업원들도 친절하기 때문에 '우리식당'에 자주
갑니다. 우진이는 비빔밥을, 민지는 된장찌개를 시켰습니다.
비빔밥에 고추장[2]이 같이 나왔는데, 우진이는 매운 음식을
싫어하기 때문에 고추장은 넣[3]지 않았습니다. 점심은 전부[4]
12,000원이었습니다. 식사 후에 민지가 점심 값을 냈습니다.
그리고 커피숍에 가서 우진이는 녹차를 마시고 민지는
커피를 마셨습니다. 이번에는 우진이가 돈을 냈습니다.

1. 이: a suffix inserted after a Korean first name that ends in a consonant
2. 고추장: red-pepper paste   3. 넣다: put in   4. 전부: altogether, in total

Exercise

Fill in the blanks based on the narration.

(1) '우리식당'은 종업원도 _____고 _____도 쌉니다.

(2) 점심에 민지는 _____을 먹고 우진이는 _____를 먹었습니다.

(3) 우진은 _____을 싫어하기 때문에 고추장은 넣지 않았습니다.

(4) 점심은 전부 _____원이었습니다.

(5) 커피숍에서 차를 마시고 우진이가 돈을 _____.

✏️ **Notes**

....

....

....

....

....

....

CULTURE

한국의 음식 문화 (Korean food culture)

The importance of rice in the Korean diet cannot be overemphasized. In fact, various terms are used to differentiate rice in different stages: rice seedlings are called 모, rice plants growing in a paddy are called 벼, processed rice without coating is called 쌀, and cooked rice ready to be served is called 밥. Considering the centrality of rice in the Korean diet, it is no coincidence that 밥 refers to an entire meal as well.

A typical Korean meal would include a bowl of rice and a bowl of soup (국). The rice is placed on the left and the soup on the right. Next to the soup are a pair of chopsticks and a spoon. In the central area of the table there are side dishes (반찬) for everyone to share. Koreans share food with each other at the same table and usually don't mind eating directly from the same dishes. It is thought to be impolite to make loud sounds when you eat, and you are encouraged not to hold your bowl of rice up to your mouth.

Even though 불고기 and 김치 might be the best-known Korean dishes to the rest of the world, the single most popular food for Koreans when they eat out is 삼겹살 (*lit.* three-layered meat). It is pork belly that has layers of marbling on one end. The most popular way to eat it is to wrap the grilled 삼겹살 in a piece of lettuce with such accoutrements as garlic, green onion, and chili. You can even add a special sauce to the wrap before you pop it into your mouth. 소주 is a popular liquor that Koreans enjoy with 삼겹살.

배달음식 (delivery food) is very popular in Korea, and you can have almost everything delivered to wherever you are. When the weather is nice, many people bring tents to the Han River (한강) in Seoul and have a picnic. One of the most popular dishes to have delivered is '치맥', which is short for "chicken and beer." Enjoying 치맥 while relaxing near the beautiful Han River is a great way to spend the weekend.

불고기

김치

USAGE

A　*Making suggestions*

>　(1)　종업원:　주문하시겠어요?
>　　　　손님:　잠깐만요. 메뉴 좀 볼게요.
>
>　(2)　종업원:　냉면 잘라 드릴까요?
>　　　　손님:　네, 잘라 주세요.
>
>　(3)　우진:　점심 뭐 먹을까요?
>　　　　마크:　오늘은 피자가 먹고 싶은데요.
>　　　　우진:　그럼, 학교 앞 피자 가게로 갈까요?

Several verbal endings may be used in making suggestions or proposals (e.g., ~(으)ㄹ까요? ~어/아 드릴까요? or ~(으)시겠어요?). The choice depends on the formality of the situation and the relationship between the speaker and the listener.

Typically the response to a suggestion is in request form with 주세요. 해 드릴까요? implies that the listener benefits from the action, and 할까요 often involves both parties doing something together.

Exercise 1

Answer the following suggestions:

(1)　불고기 드릴까요? _____

(2)　문 좀 열까요? _____

(3)　차 한 잔 사 드릴까요? _____

(4)　오늘은 댁에 일찍 들어가시겠어요? _____

(5)　비가 오는데 집에 있을까요? _____

Exercise 2

Place an order in the restaurants named below.

(1) 한국 음식점   (2) 피자 가게   (3) 커피숍

B   *Ordering food*

(1)   종업원: 주문하시겠어요?
         손님: 불고기 일 인 분 ('one portion') 주세요.
         종업원: 네, 알겠습니다. 잠깐만 기다리세요.

(2)   종업원: 여기 메뉴 있습니다.
         손님: 스파게티 ('spaghetti') 주세요.
         종업원: 마실 거는 뭘 드릴까요?
         손님: 콜라 ('cola') 주세요.

(3)   종업원: 뭐 드시겠어요?
         손님: 녹차 있어요?
         종업원: 녹차는 없는데요.
         손님: 그럼 커피 주세요.

The waiter or waitress in a restaurant usually asks:

주문하시겠어요?   지금 시키실래요?
뭐 드시겠어요?   반찬 더 갖다 드릴까요?

Exercise 1

Interview your partner; report the answers to the class.

(1) 어떤 음식을 좋아하세요? _____

(2) 보통 무슨 음료수를 마셔요? _____

(3) 어제 저녁에 뭐 먹었어요? _____

(4) 요리하는 것을 좋아하세요? (요리하다 'to cook')

   _____

(5) 어느 식당에 자주 가세요? _____

(6) 보통 어디에서 친구를 만나요? _____

(7) 한국 음식을 좋아하세요? _____

(8) 보통 어디서 점심을 먹어요? _____

(9) 학교 근처에 맛있는 식당이 어디예요? _____

(10) 어디 커피가 맛있어요? _____

Exercise 2

Here is information about two restaurants in Seoul.
Role-play with your classmate on the following topics:

(1) 삼원 가든
주소: 서울시 강남구 압구정동 신사로 111
전화 번호: (02) 548-3030, 544-5351
지하철 3호선 압구정역에서 택시로 15분

메뉴

갈비구이	₩ 29,000	불고기	₩ 22,000
국수전골	₩ 16,500	비빔밥	₩ 9,000
갈비탕	₩ 11,000	된장 찌개	₩ 8,000

(2) 우래옥
주소: 서울시 중구 무교동 무교로 111
전화 번호: (02) 265-0151/2
지하철 2호선 을지로 4가역에서 걸어서 3분

메뉴

물냉면	₩ 11,500	비빔냉면	₩ 12,000
회냉면	₩ 9,000	육회	₩ 23,000
된장 찌개	₩ 7,000	만둣국	₩ 7,000

(1) Call the restaurants and ask for their addresses, phone numbers, and directions.

(2) Call the restaurant and make a reservation for a group of 20 people. Then ask what's on the menu and order for the group.

(3) You're at the restaurant. Place an order with the waiter/waitress.

C *Describing tastes*

Exercise

Give at least two examples for each category.

(1) 단 음식: _____

(2) 짠 음식: _____

(3) 매운 음식: _____

(4) 찬 음식: _____

(5) 뜨거운 음식: _____

(6) 달고 매운 음식: _____

Notes

. . . .

. . . .

. . . .

. . . .

. . . .

. . . .

Lesson 16 At a Restaurant

CONVERSATION 1 *Have you ever tried naengmyeon?*

▌ Soobin, Soobin's mom, Woojin, and Mark enter a Korean restaurant.

Server:	Welcome. How many people are in your party?
Woojin:	There are four of us. Are there seats available?
Server:	Yes, right this way please.

▌ Everybody sits at the table. The server brings water and menus.

Server:	Would you like to place your order?
Soobin's mom:	I'd like the *bibimbap* (mixed rice dish).
Woojin:	I'll get the *sundubu jjigae* (soft tofu stew).
Soobin:	I'll have the *bulgogi* (thinly sliced bbq meat) and *naengmyeon* (cold noodles). Mark, have you tried eating *naengmyeon*?$^{G16.1}$
Mark:	Yes, I tried eating it once at the school cafeteria and it was all right. But I don't particularly like cold foods, so$^{G16.2}$ I'll have the *yukgaejang* (spicy beef stew).
Server:	Very well. I will bring everything out shortly.

CONVERSATION 2 *Isn't the yukkaejang spicy?*

▌ The server brings food.

Server:	Here's your food. Who ordered the *bibimbap*?
Soobin:	Please place it in front of my mother.
Server:	Shall I cut the *naengmyeon* for you?$^{G16.3}$
Soobin:	Yes, please.
Mark, Woojin:	Thank you for the food, (Soobin's) mother!
Soobin's mother:	Isn't the *yukgaejang* too spicy?$^{G16.4}$
Mark:	It's fine. It's very tasty. Woojin, how's the *sundubu-jjigae*?
Woojin:	It's not that salty and tastes great!
Soobin's mother:	(To the server) Excuse me, could you bring us a little more *kimchi* and side dishes?
Server:	Yes, ma'am.

▌ after a while

Mark, Woojin:	Thank you very much for a great meal!
Soobin's mother:	Excuse me. Could you bring us the check?
Server:	Yes, ma'am.

NARRATION   *Lunch*

Today, Woojin and Minji ate lunch at Woori Restaurant in front of school. In the front of the school, there are several restaurants but they often go to Woori Restaurant since the prices are inexpensive and the employees are friendly. Woojin ordered the *bibimbap*, while Minji ordered the *doenjang jjigae*. *Gochujang* came with the *bibimbap*, but because Woojin dislikes spicy food he did not use any for his meal. Lunch was ₩12,000 altogether. After they finished eating, Minji paid for their lunch. They then went to a coffee shop, where Woojin had green tea and Minji had coffee. This time Woojin paid the bill.

Appendices

Appendix 1-1 — Copula, Adjective, and Verb Conjugations

Lesson	Dictionary form / Patterns	이다	아니다	있다	계시다	되다	하다 / Adjective: 깨끗하다 / Verb: 공부하다
G12.2 G13.5	~겠어요 polite	-	-	있겠어요	계시겠어요	되겠어요	깨끗하겠어요 공부하겠어요
G7.3	~고 clausal connective	(이)고	아니고	있고	계시고	되고	깨끗하고 공부하고
G15.5	~고 나서 clausal connective	-	-	-	-	되고 나서	공부하고 나서
G10.2	~고 싶다/ 싶어 하다 expressing desire			있고 싶다 /싶어 하다	계시고 싶어 하다	되고 싶다 /싶어 하다	- 공부하고 싶다 / 싶어 하다
G11.1	~고 있다 progressive	-	-	-	-	되고 있다	- 공부하고 있다
G16.2	~기 때문에 clausal connective	(이)기 때문에	아니기 때문에	있기 때문에	계시기 때문에	되기 때문에	깨끗하기 때문에 공부하기 때문에
G9.2	~(으)ㄴ noun modifier	인	아닌	-	-	-	깨끗한 -
G12.5	~(으)ㄴ noun modifier (past)	-	-	-	계신	된	- 공부한
G10.1	~(으)ㄴ데 background information	인데	아닌데	-	-	-	깨끗한데 -
G10.5	~는 noun modifier	-	-	있는	계시는	되는	- 공부하는

Lesson	Patterns	이다	아니다	있다	계시다	되다	하다 Adjective: 깨끗하다 Verb: 공부하다
G10.1	~는데 background information	-	-	있는데	계시는데	되는데	- 공부하는데
G12.3	~네요 sentence ending	(이)네요	아니네요	있네요	계시네요	되네요	깨끗하네요 공부하네요
G15.4	~(으)ㄹ noun modifier (prospective)	일	아닐	있을	계실	될	- 공부할
G7.1	~(으)ㄹ 거예요 probability	일 거예요	아닐 거예요	있을 거예요	계실 거예요	될 거예요	깨끗할 거예요 공부할 거예요
G13.3	~(으)ㄹ게요 'I will' (willingness)	-	-	있을게요	-	될게요	- 공부할게요
G11.4	~(으)ㄹ까요? asking opinion	일까요?	아닐까요?	있을까요?	계실까요?	될까요?	깨끗할까요? 공부할까요?
G11.2	~(으)ㄹ래요 intention	-	-	있을래요 있을래요?	- 계실래요?	될래요 될래요?	- 공부할래요
G15.1	~(으)ㄹ 수 있다/없다 possibility/ ability	일 수 있다/ 없다	아닐 수 있다/없다	있을 수 있다/없다	계실 수 있다/ 없다	될 수 있다/없다	깨끗할 수 있다/없다 공부할 수 있다/없다

Lesson	Dictionary form / Patterns	이다	아니다	있다	계시다	되다	하다 Adjective: 깨끗하다 Verb: 공부하다
G5.3	~(으)러 purpose	-	-	-	-	-	- 공부하러
G15.3	~(으)면서 'while ~ing'	이면서	아니면서	있으면서	계시면서	되면서	깨끗하면서 공부하면서
G3.2	~(으)세요 honorific polite	(이)세요	아니세요	있으세요	계세요	되세요	깨끗하세요 공부하세요
G9.4	~(으)셨어요 honorific polite (past)	(이)셨어요	아니셨어요	있으셨어요	계셨어요	되셨어요	깨끗하셨어요 공부하셨어요
G8.3	~(으)셨습니다 honorific deferential (past)	(이)셨습니다	아니셨습니다	있으셨습니다	계셨습니다	되셨습니다	깨끗하셨습니다 공부하셨습니다
G8.3	~습니다/까? ~ㅂ니다/까? deferential	입니다/ 입니까?	아닙니다/ 아닙니까?	있습니다/ 있습니까?	계십니다/ 계십니까?	됩니다/ 됩니까?	깨끗합니다/ 깨끗합니까? 공부합니다/ 공부합니까?
G8.3	~(으)십니다/ (으)십니까? honorific deferential	(이)십니다/ (이)십니까?	아니십니다/ 아니십니까?	있으십니다/ 있으십니까?	계십니다/ 계십니까?	되십니다/ 되십니까?	깨끗하십니다/ 깨끗하십니까? 공부하십니다/ 공부하십니까?
G16.1	~어/아 보다 'try doing'	-	-	있어 보다	계셔 보다	되어 보다 /돼 보다	- 공부해 보다
G10.4 G12.1	~어서/아서 causal, sequential clausal conn.	(이)라서 /이어서 /여서	아니라서/ 아니어서	있어서	계셔서	되어서 /돼서	깨끗해서 공부해서
G2.5	~어요/아요 polite	이에요 /예요	아니에요	있어요	계세요	되어요 /돼요	깨끗해요 공부해요

Lesson	Patterns	이다	아니다	있다	계시다	되다	하다 Adjective: 깨끗하다 Verb: 공부하다
	Dictionary form						
G13.2	~어/아야 되다 obligation, necessity	이어야/여야 되다	아니어야 되다	있어야 되다	계셔야 되다	되어야 되다 /돼야 되다	깨끗해야 되다 공부해야 되다
G13.1	~어/아 주다 /드리다 benefactive	-	-	있어 주다 /드리다	계셔 주다	되어 주다 /드리다	- 공부해 주다 /드리다
G10.1	~었/았는데 background information (past)	이었는데 /였는데	아니었는데	있었는데	계셨는데	되었는데	깨끗했는데 공부했는데
G8.3	~었/았습니다 deferential (past)	이었습니다 /였습니다	아니었습니다	있었습니다	계셨습니다	되었습니다	깨끗했습니다 공부했습니다
G6.3	~었/았/ㅆ어요 polite (past)	이었어요 /였어요	아니었어요	있었어요	계셨어요	되었어요	깨끗했어요 공부했어요
G14.4	~지 마세요 negative command	-	-	있지 마세요	계시지 마세요	되지 마세요	- 공부하지 마세요
G9.5	~지만 'but, although'	(이)지만	아니지만	있지만	계시지만	되지만	깨끗하지만 공부하지만
G14.2	~지 못하다 'cannot' long negation	-	-	있지 못하다	계시지 못하다	되지 못하다	깨끗하지 못하다 공부하지 못하다
G16.4	~지 않다 'do not' long negation	-	-	있지 않다	계시지 않다	되지 않다	깨끗하지 않다 공부하지 않다
G8.1	~지요? seeking agreement	(이)지요?	아니지요?	있지요?	계시지요?	되지요?	깨끗하지요? 공부하지요?

Appendix 1-2 | Conjugation of Irregular Adjectives and Verbs

Lesson	Dictionary form / Patterns	-ㄷ 듣다 걷다 묻다	-ㄹ Adjective: 멀다, 길다 / Verb: 열다, 팔다, 놀다, 돌다, 만들다, 살다, 알다	-ㅂ Adjective: 춥다, 덥다, 쉽다, 어렵다, 반갑다, 즐겁다 / Verb: 돕다
G12.2 G13.2	~겠어요 polite	듣겠어요	멀겠어요 / 열겠어요	춥겠어요 / 돕겠어요
G7.3	~고 clausal connective	듣고	멀고 / 열고	춥고 / 돕고
G15.5	~고 나서 clausal connective	듣고 나서	- / 열고 나서	돕고 나서
G10.2	~고 싶다/싶어 하다 expressing desire	듣고 싶다 듣고 싶어 하다	- / 열고 싶다 열고 싶어 하다	돕고 싶다 돕고 싶어 하다
G11.1	~고 있다 progressive	듣고 있다	- / 열고 있다	돕고 있다
G16.2	~기 때문에 clausal connective	듣기 때문에	멀기 때문에 / 열기 때문에	춥기 때문에 / 돕기 때문에
G9.2	~(으)ㄴ noun modifier	-	먼 / -	추운 / -
G12.5	~(으)ㄴ noun modifier (past)	들은	- / 연	- / 도운
G10.1	~(으)ㄴ데 background information	-	먼데 / -	추운데 / -
G10.5	~는 noun modifier	듣는	- / 여는	- / 돕는

Lesson	Dictionary form / Patterns	~ㅎ 그렇다 이렇다 저렇다 빨갛다 노랗다 파랗다 하얗다	~으 Adjective: 크다, 바쁘다 Verb: 쓰다	~르 Adjective: 다르다, 빠르다 Verb: 부르다, 모르다
G12.2 G13.2	~겠어요 polite	그렇겠어요	크겠어요 쓰겠어요	다르겠어요 부르겠어요
G7.3	~고 clausal connective	그렇고	크고 쓰고	다르고 부르고
G15.5	~고 나서 clausal connective	그러고 나서	- 쓰고 나서	부르고 나서
G10.2	~고 싶다/싶어 하다 expressing desire	그러고 싶다/ 그러고 싶어 하다	- 쓰고 싶다/ 쓰고 싶어 하다	- 부르고 싶다/ 부르고 싶어 하다
G11.1	~고 있다 progressive	그러고 있다	- 쓰고 있다	- 부르고 있다
G16.3	~기 때문에 clausal connective	그렇기 때문에	크기 때문에 쓰기 때문에	다르기 때문에 부르기 때문에
G9.2	Adjective ~(으)ㄴ noun modifier	그런	큰 -	다른 -
G12.5	Verb ~(으)ㄴ noun modifier (past)	-	- 쓴	- 부른
G10.1	Adjective ~(으)ㄴ데 background information	그런데	큰데 -	다른데 -
G10.5	Verb ~는 noun modifier	-	- 쓰는	- 부르는

Lesson	Patterns	Dictionary form - ㄷ 듣다 걷다 묻다	- ㄹ Adjective: 멀다, 길다 Verb: 열다, 팔다, 놀다, 돌다, 만들다, 살다, 알다	- ㅂ Adjective: 춥다, 덥다, 쉽다, 어렵다, 반갑다, 즐겁다 Verb: 돕다
G10.1	~는데 background information	듣는데	- 여는데	- 돕는데
G12.3	~네요 sentence ending	듣네요	머네요 여네요	춥네요 돕네요
G15.4	~(으)ㄹ noun modifier (prospective)	들을	멀 열	추울 도울
G7.1	~(으)ㄹ 거예요 probability	들을 거예요	멀 거예요 열 거예요	추울 거예요 도울 거예요
G13.3	~(으)ㄹ게요 'I will' (willingness)	들을게요	- 열게요	- 도울게요
G11.4	~(으)ㄹ까요? asking opinion	들을까요?	멀까요? 열까요?	추울까요? 도울까요?
G11.2	~(으)ㄹ래요 intention	들을래요	- 열래요	- 도울래요
G15.1	~(으)ㄹ 수 있다/없다 possibility/ability	들을 수 있다	- 열 수 있다	- 도울 수 있다

Lesson	Dictionary form / Patterns	-ㅎ 그렇다 이렇다 저렇다 빨갛다 노랗다 파랗다 하얗다	-으 Adjective: 크다, 바쁘다 / Verb: 쓰다	-르 Adjective: 다르다, 빠르다 / Verb: 부르다, 모르다
G10.1	~는데 background information	그런데	- 쓰는데	- 부르는데
G12.3	~네요 sentence ending	그렇네요	크네요 쓰네요	다르네요 부르네요
G15.4	~(으)ㄹ noun modifier (prospective)	그럴	클 쓸	다를 부를
G7.1	~(으)ㄹ 거예요 probability	그럴 거예요	클 거예요 쓸 거예요	다를 거예요 부를 거예요
G13.3	~(으)ㄹ게요 'I will' (willingness)	그럴게요	- 쓸게요	- 부를게요
G11.4	~(으)ㄹ까요? asking opinion	그럴까요?	클까요? 쓸까요?	다를까요? 부를까요?
G11.2	~(으)ㄹ래요 intention	그럴래요	- 쓸래요	- 부를래요
G15.1	~(으)ㄹ 수 있다/없다 possibility/ability	그럴 수 있다	클 수 있다 쓸 수 있다	다를 수 있다 부를 수 있다

Lesson	Dictionary form / Patterns	-ㄷ 듣다 걷다 묻다	-ㄹ Adjective: 멀다, 길다 / Verb: 열다, 팔다, 놀다, 돌다, 만들다, 살다, 알다	-ㅂ Adjective: 춥다, 덥다, 쉽다, 어렵다, 반갑다, 즐겁다 / Verb: 돕다
G5.3	~(으)러 purpose	들으러	- 열러	- 도우러
G15.3	~(으)면서 'while ~ing'	들으면서	멀면서 열면서	추우면서 도우면서
G3.2	~(으)세요 honorific polite	들으세요	머세요 여세요	추우세요 도우세요
G9.4	~(으)셨어요 honorific polite (past)	들으셨어요	머셨어요 여셨어요	추우셨어요 도우셨어요
G8.3	~(으)셨습니다 honorific deferential (past)	들으셨습니다	- 여셨습니다	- 도우셨습니다
G8.3	~습니다/까? ~ㅂ니다/까? deferential	들습니다/까?	멉니다/까? 엽니다/까?	춥습니다/까? 도웁니다/까?
G8.3	~(으)십니다/ (으)십니까? honorific deferential	들으십니다/까?	머십니다/까? 여십니다/까?	추우십니다/까? 도우십니다/까?
G16.1	~어/아 보다 'try doing'	들어 보다	- 열어 보다	- 도와 보다
G10.4 G12.1	~어서/아서 causal, sequential clausal conn.	들어서	멀어서 열어서	추워서 도와서

	Dictionary form	-ㅎ	-으	-르
Lesson	Patterns	그렇다 이렇다 저렇다 빨갛다 노랗다 파랗다 하얗다	Adjective: 크다, 바쁘다 Verb: 쓰다	Adjective: 다르다, 빠르다 Verb: 부르다, 모르다
G5.3	~(으)러 purpose	-	- 쓰러	- 부르러
G15.3	~(으)면서 'while ~ing'	그러면서	크면서 쓰면서	다르면서 부르면서
G3.2	~(으)세요 honorific polite	그러세요	크세요 쓰세요	- 부르세요
G9.4	~(으)셨어요 honorific polite (past)	그러셨어요	크셨어요 쓰셨어요	다르셨어요 부르셨어요
G8.3	~(으)셨습니다 honorific deferential (past)	그러셨습니다	크셨습니다 쓰셨습니다	다르셨습니다 부르셨습니다
G8.3	~습니다/까? ~ㅂ니다/까? deferential	그렇습니다/까?	크셨습니다/까? 쓰셨습니다/까?	다릅니다/까? 부릅니다/까?
G8.3	~(으)십니다/ (으)십니까? honorific deferential	그러십니다/까?	크십니다/까? 쓰십니다/까?	다르십니다/까? 부르십니다/까?
G16.1	~어/아 보다 'try doing'	그래 보다	- 써 보다	- 불러 보다
G10.4 G12.1	~어서/아서 causal, sequential clausal conn.	그래서	커서 써서	달라서 불러서

Lesson	Dictionary form / Patterns	-ㄷ 듣다 걷다 묻다	-ㄹ Adjective: 멀다, 길다 Verb: 열다, 팔다, 놀다, 돌다, 만들다, 살다, 알다	-ㅂ Adjective: 춥다, 덥다, 쉽다, 어렵다, 반갑다, 즐겁다 Verb: 돕다
G2.5	~어요/아요 polite	들어요	멀어요 열어요	추워요 도와요
G13.2	~어/아야 되다 obligation, necessity	들어야 되다	멀어야 되다 열어야 되다	추워야 되다 도와야 되다
G13.1	~어/아 주다 /드리다 benefactive	들어 주다/드리다	- 열어 주다/드리다	- 도와 주다/드리다
G10.1	~었/았는데 background information (past)	들었는데	멀었는데 열었는데	추웠는데 도왔는데
G8.3	~었/았습니다 deferential (past)	들었습니다	멀었습니다 열었습니다	추웠습니다 도왔습니다
G6.3	~었/았/ㅆ어요 polite (past)	들었어요	멀었어요 열었어요	추웠어요 도왔어요
G14.4	~지 마세요 negative command	듣지 마세요	- 열지 마세요	- 돕지 마세요
G9.5	~지만 'but, although'	듣지만	멀지만 열지만	춥지만 돕지만
G14.2	~지 못하다 'cannot' long negation	듣지 못하다	- 열지 못하다	- 돕지 못하다
G16.4	~지 않다 'do not' long negation	듣지 않다	멀지 않다 열지 않다	춥지 않다 돕지 않다
G8.1	~지요? seeking agreement	듣지요?	멀지요? 열지요?	춥지요? 돕지요?

Lesson	Dictionary form / Patterns	-ㅎ 그렇다 이렇다 저렇다 빨갛다 노랗다 파랗다 하얗다	-으 Adjective: 크다, 바쁘다 / Verb: 쓰다	-르 Adjective: 다르다, 빠르다 / Verb: 부르다, 모르다
G2.5	~어요/아요 polite	그래요	커요 / 써요	달라요 / 불러요
G13.2	~어/아야 되다 obligation, necessity	그래야 돼요	커야 돼요 / 써야 돼요	달라야 돼요 / 불러야 돼요
G13.1	~어/아 주다 /드리다 benefactive	-	- / 써 주다/드리다	- / 불러 주다/드리다
G10.1	~었/았는데 background information (past)	그랬는데	컸는데 / 썼는데	달랐는데 / 불렀는데
G8.3	~었/았습니다 deferential (past)	그랬습니다	컸습니다 / 썼습니다	달랐습니다 / 불렀습니다
G6.3	~었/았/ㅆ어요 polite (past)	그랬어요	컸어요 / 썼어요	달랐어요 / 불렀어요
G14.4	~지 마세요 negative command	그러지 마세요	- / 쓰지 마세요	- / 부르지 마세요
G9.5	~지만 'but, although'	그렇지만	크지만 / 쓰지만	다르지만 / 부르지만
G14.2	~지 못하다 'cannot' long negation	그렇지 못하다	- / 쓰지 못하다	- / 부르지 못하다
G16.4	~지 않다 'do not' long negation	그렇지 않다	크지 않다 / 쓰지 않다	다르지 않다 / 부르지 않다
G8.1	~지요? seeking agreement	그렇지요?	크지요? / 쓰지요?	다르지요? / 부르지요?

Appendix 1-3   The Three Types of Conjugation

Conjugations for adjectives and verbs can be classified into the following three types:

A. stem + 어/아
B. stem + (으)
C. no change in stem

A. Stem + 어/아	B. Stem + (으)	C. No change in stem
~어/아 드리다	~(으)ㄴ	~게
~어/아 보다	~(으)ㄴ데	~겠
~어/아 주다	~(으)ㄴ데요	~고
~어/아야 되다	~(으)ㄹ	~고 나서
~어서/아서	~(으)ㄹ 거예요	~(스)ㅂ니다
~어요/아요	~(으)ㄹ 수	~(스)ㅂ니까
~었/았/ㅆ어요	~(으)ㄹ게요	~고 싶다
	~(으)ㄹ까요?	~고 있다
	~(으)ㄹ래요(?)	~기
	~(으)러	~기 때문에
	~(으)면서	~네요
	~(으)세요	~는
	~(으)시	~는데
		~는데요
		~지만
		~지 말다
		~지 못하다
		~지 않다
		~지요

Appendix 2   Kinship Terms

1. 가족 'family'; 식구 'member of a family'

부모	parents	맏아들	first son
부모님	parents *hon.*	외(동)아들	only son
아버지	father	딸	daughter *plain*
아버님	father *hon.*	따님	daughter *hon.*
어머니	mother	맏딸	first daughter
어머님	mother *hon.*	외(동)딸	only daughter
할아버지	grandfather	형제	sibling(s)
할아버님	grandfather *hon.*	형	male's older brother
할머니	grandmother	형님	male's older brother *hon.*
할머님	grandmother *hon.*	누나	male's older sister
남편	husband	누님	male's older sister *hon.*
아내	wife *plain*	오빠	female's older brother
부인	wife *hon.*	언니	female's older sister
아들	son *plain*	남동생	younger brother
아드님	son *hon.*	여동생	younger sister
		막내	youngest child

2. 친척 'relative(s)'

아저씨	uncle
아주머니	aunt
큰아버지	uncle (who is one's father's older brother)
큰어머니	aunt (who is the wife of one's father's older brother)
작은아버지	uncle (who is one's father's younger brother)
작은어머니	aunt (who is the wife of one's father's younger brother)
삼촌	uncle (who is one's father's younger brother)
숙모	aunt (who is the wife of one's father's younger brother)
외삼촌	uncle (who is one's mother's brother)
외숙모	aunt (who is the wife of one's mother's brother)
고모	aunt (who is one's father's sister)
이모	aunt (who is one's mother's sister)
사촌	cousin

Appendix 3   Numbers

Arabic numeral	Sino-Korean	Native Korean	Native Korean before counters
0	영 or 공	-	-
1	일	하나	**한**
2	이	둘	**두**
3	삼	셋	**세**
4	사	넷	**네**
5	오	다섯	다섯
6	육	여섯	여섯
7	칠	일곱	일곱
8	팔	여덟	여덟
9	구	아홉	아홉
10	십	열	열
11	십일	열하나	열한
12	십이	열둘	열두
13	십삼	열셋	열세
14	십사	열넷	열네
15	십오	열다섯	열다섯
16	십육 [심뉵]	열여섯	열여섯
17	십칠	열일곱	열일곱
18	십팔	열여덟	열여덟
19	십구	열아홉	열아홉
20	이십	스물	스무
30	삼십	서른	서른
40	사십	마흔	마흔
50	오십	쉰	쉰
60	육십	예순	예순
70	칠십	일흔	일흔
80	팔십	여든	여든
90	구십	아흔	아흔
100	백		
1,000	천		
10,000	만		

Large Numbers

100	백	200	이백
1,000	천	2,000	이천
10,000	만	20,000	이만
100,000	십만	200,000	이십만
1,000,000	백만	2,000,000	이백만
10,000,000	천만	20,000,000	이천만
100,000,000	억	200,000,000	이억
1,000,000,000	십억	2,000,000,000	이십억
10,000,000,000	백억	20,000,000,000	이백억
100,000,000,000	천억	200,000,000,000	이천억
1,000,000,000,000	조	2,000,000,000,000	이조

Appendix 4   Counters

A. With Sino-Korean numbers

Counters	What is being counted					
	층	분	과	년	월	일
	Floors of a building	Minutes	Lessons (in order)	Years	Months	Days
1	일 층	일 분	일 과	일 년	일 월	일 일
2	이 층	이 분	이 과	이 년	이 월	이 일
3	삼 층	삼 분	삼 과	삼 년	삼 월	삼 일
4	사 층	사 분	사 과	사 년	사 월	사 일
5	오 층	오 분	오 과	오 년	오 월	오 일
6	육 층	육 분	육 과	육 년	**유 월**	육 일
10	십 층	십 분	십 과	십 년	**시 월**	십 일
12	십이 층	십이 분	십이 과	십이 년	십이 월	십이 일

Counters	What is being counted					
	달러(불)	원	마일	학년	번	주일
	Dollars	Won (Korean currency)	Miles	School years	Numbers (serial)	Weeks
1	일 달러	일 원	일 마일	일학년	일 번	일 주일
2	이 달러	이 원	이 마일	이학년	이 번	이 주일
3	삼 달러	삼 원	삼 마일	삼학년	삼 번	삼 주일
4	사 달러	사 원	사 마일	사학년	사 번	사 주일
5	오 달러	오 원	오 마일	오학년	오 번	오 주일
6	육 달러	육 원	육 마일	육학년	육 번	육 주일
10	십 달러	십 원	십 마일	십학년	십 번	십 주일
12	십이 달러	십이 원	십이 마일	십이학년	십이 번	십이 주일

B. With Native Korean numbers

					What is being counted			
Counters	명	분	시	시간	달	마리	살	과목
	People	People (*hon.*)	Point of time: 'the hour'	Duration: 'hours'	Duration: 'months'	Animals	Age: 'years old'	Academic subjects
1	한 명	한 분	한 시	한 시간	한 달	한 마리	한 살	한 과목
2	두 명	두 분	두 시	두 시간	두 달	두 마리	두 살	두 과목
3	세 명	세 분	세 시	세 시간	세 달	세 마리	세 살	세 과목
4	네 명	네 분	네 시	네 시간	네 달	네 마리	네 살	네 과목
5	다섯 명	다섯 분	다섯 시	다섯 시간	다섯 달	다섯 마리	다섯 살	다섯 과목
6	여섯 명	여섯 분	여섯 시	여섯 시간	여섯 달	여섯 마리	여섯 살	여섯 과목
10	열 명	열 분	열 시	열 시간	열 달	열 마리	열 살	열 과목

				What is being counted				
Counters	과	개	권	장	병	잔	번	대
	Number of lessons	Items	Volumes	Sheets (of paper)	Bottles	Cups and glasses	Times	Vehicles, cars
1	한 과	한 개	한 권	한 장	한 병	한 잔	한 번	한 대
2	두 과	두 개	두 권	두 장	두 병	두 잔	두 번	두 대
3	세 과	세 개	세 권	세 장	세 병	세 잔	세 번	세 대
4	네 과	네 개	네 권	네 장	네 병	네 잔	네 번	네 대
5	다섯 과	다섯 개	다섯 권	다섯 장	다섯 병	다섯 잔	다섯 번	다섯 대
6	여섯 과	여섯 개	여섯 권	여섯 장	여섯 병	여섯 잔	여섯 번	여섯 대
10	열 과	열 개	열 권	열 장	열 병	열 잔	열 번	열 대

Grammar Index

L = lesson, C = conversation, G = grammar

Korean-English Glossary

Korean	English
1학년	freshman
2학년	sophomore
3학년	junior
4학년	senior
가	subject particle
가게	store
가깝다	to be close, near
가끔	sometimes
가다	to go
가르치다	to teach
가방	bag
가수	singer
가운데	the middle, the center
가위, 바위, 보	rock-paper-scissors
가을	autumn, fall
가장	the most
가족	family
갈비	galbi (barbecued spareribs)
갈아 입다	to change (clothes)
갈아 타다	to change (vehicles)
감기에 걸리다	to have, catch a cold
감사하다	to be thankful
값	price
갖고 가다	to take
갖고 다니다	to carry around
갖고 오다	to bring
갖다 놓다	to bring and put down somewhere
갖다 드리다 hum.	to bring/take something to someone
갖다 주다	to bring/take something to someone
같이	together
개1	dog
개2	item (counter)
거	thing (contraction of 것)
거기	there
거리1	distance
거리2	street
건강하다	to be healthy
건너다	to cross
건너편	the other side
건물	building
건축학	architecture
걷다	to walk
걸리다	to take [time]
걸어가다	to go on foot
걸어다니다	to walk around
걸어오다	to come on foot
것	thing (=거)
게임	game
겨울	winter
결혼	marriage
결혼하다	to get married
경기	match, game
경제학	economics
계단	stairs
계산서	check
계시다 hon.	to be (existence), stay
계절	season
계획	plan
계획하다	to plan
고등학교	high school
고등학생	high school student
고르다	to choose, select
고맙다	to be thankful
고장	breakdown
고추장	red-pepper paste
고향	hometown
골프	golf
곳	place
공	0 (zero: for phone #)
공부	study
공부하다	to study
공원	park
공포 영화	horror movie
공항	airport
과1	lesson, chapter
과2	and (joins nouns) (narration only)
과목	course, subject
과일	fruit
과자	cracker
괜찮다	to be all right, okay
굉장히	very much
교과서	textbook
교수님	professor
교실	classroom
교육학	education
교통	traffic
교회	church
구경하다	to look around; to sightsee
구두 시험	oral exam

귀걸이	earring	나 *plain*	I (=저 *hum.*)
군데	place, spot	나가다	to go out
권	volume (counter)	나다	happen, break out
그	that	나라	country
그냥	just, without any special reason	나쁘다	to be bad
		나오다	to come out
그동안	meantime	나이	age
그래서	so, therefore	나중에	later
그런데	1. but, however; 2. by the way	날	day
		날마다	every day
그럼	(if so) then	날씨	weather
그렇다	to be so	남기다	to leave (a message)
그렇지만	but, however	남동생	younger brother
그리고	and	남자	man
그리다	to draw	내 *plain*	my (=제 *hum.*)
그림	picture, painting	내년	next year
그만	without doing anything further	(돈을)내다	to pay
		내려가다	to go down
극장	movie theater	내리다	to get off
근처	nearby, vicinity	내일	tomorrow
글쎄요	Well; It's hard to say	냉면	*naengmyeon* (cold buckwheat noodles)
금반지	gold ring		
금방	soon	너	you
금요일	Friday	너무	too much
기계 공학	mechanical engineering	넓다	to be spacious, wide
기다리다	to wait	네	1. yes;
기분	feeling		2. I see;
기사	driver		3. okay
기숙사	dormitory	년	year (counter)
기차	train	노랗다	to be yellow
기타	guitar	노래	song
길	street, road	노래 부르다	to sing
길다	to be long	노래방	karaoke room
김밥	*gimbap*	녹차	green tea
김치	*kimchi*	놀다	to play; to not work
까만색	black (=까망)	농구	basketball
까맣다	to be black	농구 시합	basketball game
까지	1. up to (location); 2. to/until/through (time); 3. including	놓아 주다	to put something down for someone
		누가	who (누구+가)
깨끗하다	to be clean	누구	who
께 *hon.*	to (a person)	누나	the older sister of a male
께서 *hon.*	subject particle (=이/가 *plain*)	눈1	eyes
		눈2	snow
꽃	flower	눈(이) 오다	to snow
꽃집	flower shop	뉴스	news
꿈(을) 꾸다	to dream a dream	뉴욕	New York
끝나다	to be over, finished	는	topic particle ('as for')
끼다	to wear (glasses, gloves, rings)	늦게	late
		늦다	to be late

늦잠	oversleep	동네	neighborhood
다	all	동대문시장	East Gate Market
다니다	to attend	동부	East Coast
다르다	to be different	동생	younger sibling
다시	again	동안	during
다음	next, following	동양학	Asian studies
다음부터(는)	from next time	되다	to become, get, turn into
달	month (counter)	된장찌개	soybean-paste stew
달다	to be sweet	두	two (with counter)
달러	dollar (=불)	두 번째	the second
닮다	to resemble	둘	two
담배	cigarette	뒤	the back, behind
답	answer	드라마	drama
대답	answer	드럼	drum
대답하다	to answer	드리다 *hum.*	to give (=주다 *plain*)
대통령	president	드시다 *hon.*	to eat (=먹다 *plain*)
대통령 선거	presidential election	듣다	1. to listen;
대학	college, university		2. to take a course
대학교	college, university	들	plural particle
대학생	college student	들어가다	to enter
대학원	graduate school	들어오다	to come in
대학원생	graduate student	등	et cetera
댁 *hon.*	home, house (=집 *plain*)	등산	hiking
더	more	등산하다	to hike
더럽다	to be dirty	따님 *hon.*	daughter
덜	less	따뜻하다	to be warm
덥다	to be hot	따라하다	to repeat after
덮다	to close, cover	딸	daughter
데	place	때	time
데이트 (하다)	to date	때문에	because of
도	also, too	또	and, also, too
도서관	library	똑바로	straight, upright
도시	city	뛰다	to run
도착하다	to arrive	뜨겁다	to be hot
도쿄	Tokyo	뜻하다	to mean, signify
독서	reading	라디오	radio
돈	money	라면	instant noodles (ramen)
돈이 들다	to cost money	라운지	lounge
돈을 내다	to pay	랩	lab
돈을 벌다	to earn money	러시아	Russia
돌	the first birthday	로스앤젤레스	Los Angeles (L.A.)
돌다	to turn	록	rock music
돌려 드리다 *hum.*	to return (something to someone)	룸메이트	roommate
		를	object particle
돌려 주다	to return (something to someone)	마리	animal (counter)
		마시다	to drink
돌아가시다 *hon.*	to pass away	마중 나가다	to go out to greet someone
돌아오다	to return, come back	마중 나오다	to come out to greet someone
돕다	to help		

마켓	market
막내	youngest child
막히다	to be blocked, congested
만	only
만나다	to meet
만들다	to make
만화책	comic book
많다	to be many, much
많이	much, many
말	speech, words
말씀 *hon.*	speech, words (=말 *plain*)
말하다	to speak
맛없다	to be tasteless, not delicious
맛있다	to be delicious
매년	every year
매달	every month
매일	every day
매주	every week
맵다	to be spicy
머리	1. head; 2. hair
먹다	to eat
멀다	to be far
메뉴	menu
메시지	message
멕시코	Mexico
며칠	what date; a few days
명	people (counter)
몇	how many, what (with a counter)
모두	all
모레	the day after tomorrow
모르다	to not know, be unaware of
모으다	to collect
모자	cap, hat
목(이) 마르다	to be thirsty
목걸이	necklace
목소리	voice
목요일	Thursday
목욕	bath
목욕하다	to bathe
몸	body
몸조리	care of health
못	cannot
무섭다	to be scary; scared
무슨	what, what kind of
무엇	what (=뭐)

무척	very much
문	door
문학	literature
문화	culture
묻다	to ask
물	water
물가	cost of living
물건	merchandise
물리학	physics
물어보다	to inquire
뭐	what (=무엇)
미국	the United States
미안하다	to be sorry
밑	the bottom, below
바꾸다	to change, switch
바닷가	beach
바쁘다	to be busy
바이올린	violin
바지	pants
박스	box
밖	outside
밖에	nothing but, only
반	half
반1	class
반2	half
반갑다	to be glad
반지	ring
반찬	side dishes
받다	to receive
발	foot
밤	night
밥	1. cooked rice; 2. meal
방	room
방학	school vacation
배	stomach, abdomen
배(가) 고프다	to be hungry
배(가) 부르다	to have a full stomach
배우다	to learn
백만	million
백화점	department store
밴쿠버	Vancouver
버스	bus
번	1. number (counter); 2. number of times (e.g., 한 번)
번째	ordinal numbers
번호	number
벌다	to earn (money)

벌써	already	사다	to buy
법학	law	사람	person, people
벗다	to take off, undress	사랑하다	to love
별로	not really/particularly	사모님	teacher's wife
보내다1	to spend time	사이	1. relationship;
보내다2	to send		2. between
보다	than	사이즈	size
보다	to see, look, watch	사전	dictionary
보스톤	Boston	사진	photo, picture
보이다	to be seen, visible	살	years old
보통	usually	살다	to live
복	good fortune	삼	3
복습	review	상	table
복잡하다	to be crowded	새	new
볼링	bowling	새로	newly
볼펜	ballpoint pen	새벽	dawn
봄	spring	새해	New Year
뵙다 *hum.*	to see (=보다 *plain*)	색	color (=색깔)
부르다 (노래)	to sing (a song)	샌드위치	sandwich
부모님	parents	생물학	biology
부엌	kitchen	생신 *hon.*	birthday
부자	a wealthy person	생일	birthday
부치다	to mail (a letter, parcel)	생활	daily life, living
부탁하다	to ask a favor	샤워	shower
부터	from (time) . . .	샤워하다	to take a shower
분	minute (counter)	서로	each other
분 *hon.*	people (=명 *plain*)	서비스	service
불	dollar (=달러)	서울	Seoul
불고기	*bulgogi* (roast meat)	서점	bookstore (=책방)
불편하다	to be uncomfortable, inconvenient	선물	present, gift
		선물하다	to give a present, gift
브로드웨이 극장	Broadway Theater	선생님	teacher
비	rain	설거지	dishwashing
비(가) 오다	to rain	설거지하다	to wash dishes
비빔밥	*bibimbap* (rice with vegetables and beef)	설악산	Seol-ak Mount
		성격	personality
비싸다	to be expensive	성함 *hon.*	name (=이름 *plain*)
비행기	airplane	세수하다	to wash one's face
빌딩	building	세일	sale
빌려주다	to lend	센트	cent
빌리다	to borrow	셔츠	shirt
빠르다	to be fast	소설	novel
빨갛다	to be red	손(을) 씻다	to wash one's hands
빨래하다	to do the laundry	손님	guest, customer
빨리	fast, quickly	쇼핑	shopping
사	4	쇼핑하다	to shop
사거리	intersection	수고하다	to put forth effort, take trouble
사고	accident		
사귀다	to make friends	수도	capital (city)

수업	course, class	싶다	to want to
수영	swimming	싸다	to be cheap
수영장	swimming pool	쓰다	1. to write;
수영하다	to swim		2. to use;
수요일	Wednesday		3. to wear headgear;
숙제	homework		4. to be bitter
숙제하다	to do homework	씨	attached to a person's
순두부찌개	soft tofu stew		name for courtesy
쉬다	to rest	아	oh
쉽다	to be easy	아니다	to not be (negative
슈퍼	supermarket		equation)
스릴러	thriller	아니요	no
스웨터	sweater	아들	son
스키	ski	아마	probably, perhaps
스키 타다	to ski	아버지	father
스트레스	stress	아이	child
스파게티	spaghetti	아이스하키	ice hockey
스페인	Spain	아저씨	mister; a man of one's
스포츠	sports		parents' age
슬프다	to be sad	아주	very, really
시1	hour, o'clock	아직	yet, still
시간	time, hour (duration)	아침	1. breakfast;
시계	clock, watch		2. morning
시끄럽다	to be noisy	아파트	apartment
시다	to be sour	아프다	to be sick
시드니	Sydney	악기	musical instrument
시원하다	to be cool, refreshing	안1	the inside
시작하다	to begin	안2	do not
시장	marketplace	안경	eyeglasses
시청	city hall	안녕하다	to be well
시청역	city hall station	안녕히	in peace
시카고	Chicago	안부	regards
시키다	to order (food)	앉다	to sit
시험	test, exam	않다	to not be, to not do
식당	restaurant	알다	to know
식사	meal	알아보다	to find out, check out
식사하다	to have a meal	앞	the front
신나다	to be excited	액션	action
신다	to wear (footwear)	야구	baseball
신문	newspaper	약국	drugstore
신발	shoes	약속	1. engagement;
신호등	traffic light		2. promise
실	thread	양말	socks, stockings
실례하다	to be excused	양식	Western-style (food)
싫다	to be undesirable	얘기	talk, chat (=이야기)
싫어하다	to dislike	얘기하다	to talk, chat
심리학	psychology	어	oh
심심하다	to be bored	어느	which
싱겁다	to be bland	어디	what place, where

어떤	which, what kind of	연주	to perform on a musical instrument
어떻게	how		
어떻다	to be how	연필	pencil
어렵다	to be difficult	열다	to open
어리다	to be young	열심히	diligently
어머	Oh! Oh my! Dear me!	영	0 (zero)
어머니	mother	영국	the United Kingdom
어서	quick(ly)	영어	the English language
어제	yesterday	영화	movie
어젯밤	last night	옆	the side, beside
언니	the older sister of a female	예	yes, I see, okay (=네)
		예쁘다	to be pretty
언어학	linguistics	오늘	today
언제	when	오다	to come
얼굴	face	오래	long time
얼마	how long/much	오래간만	after a long time
얼마나	how long/much	오른쪽	right side
엄마	mom	오빠	the older brother of a female
없다	1. to not be (existence); 2. to not have		
		오전	a.m.
에	1. in, at, on (static location); 2. to (destination); 3. at, in, on (time); 4. for, per	오후	afternoon
		올라가다	to go up
		올림	Sincerely yours
		올림픽	Olympic
		올해	this year
에서	1. in, at (dynamic location); 2. from (location); 3. from (time)	옷	clothes
		옷가게	clothing store
		와	and (joins nouns) (narration only)
엘리베이터	elevator	왜	why
여기	here	외식하다	to eat out
여동생	younger sister	왼쪽	left side
여러	many, several	요리	cooking
여름	summer	요리하다	to cook
여보	honey, dear	요즘	these days
여보세요	hello (on the phone)	우리 *plain*	we/us/our (=저희 *hum.*)
여자	woman	우산	umbrella
여자 친구	girlfriend	우체국	post office
여행	travel	우표	stamp
여행하다	to travel	운동	exercise
역	station	운동장	playground
역사	history	운동하다	to exercise
연구실	professor's office	운동화	sports shoes, sneakers
연극	play	운전하다	to drive
연락	contact	원 (₩)	won (Korean currency)
연세 *hon.*	age	월	month (counter)
연습	practice	월드컵	World Cup
연습하다	to practice	월요일	Monday
연주	musical performance	웬일	what matter

위	the top side, above
유니온 빌딩	Union Building
육개장	hot shredded beef soup
으로1	by means of
으로2	toward, to
은	topic particle ('as for')
은행	bank
을	object particle
음료수	beverage
음식	food
음식점	restaurant (=식당)
음악	music
음악회	concert
의	of
의사	doctor
의자	chair
이1	2
이2	subject particle
이3	this
이4	a suffix inserted after a Korean first name that ends in a consonant
이5	tooth
이거	this (=이것)
이기다	to win
이다	to be (equation)
이(를) 닦다	to brush one's teeth
이따가	a little later
이름	name
이메일	email
이번	this time
이사하다	to move
이스트 홀	East Hall
이야기	talk, chat (=얘기)
이야기하다	to talk (=얘기하다)
이젠	now (이제+는)
이쪽으로	this way + 으로
이태리	Italy
인구	population
인사	greeting
인사하다	to greet
인천	Incheon
인터넷	internet
인터뷰	interview
일1	1
일2	day (counter)
일3	work
일4	event
일 인 분	one portion

일본	Japan
일식	Japanese-style (food)
일어나다	to get up
일요일	Sunday
일찍	early
일하다	to work
읽다	to read
입구	entrance
입다	to wear, put on (clothes)
있다	1. to be (existence); 2. to have
자다	to sleep
자라다	to grow up
자르다	to cut
자리	seat
자전거	bicycle
자주	often, frequently
작년	last year
작다	to be small (in size)
잔	glass, cup
잔치	feast, party
잘	well
잘라 드리다 *hum.*	to cut (something for someone)
잘라 주다	to cut (something for someone)
잠	sleep
잠깐만	for a short time
잡다	to catch, grab
잡지	magazine
장(을) 보다	to buy one's groceries
장갑	gloves
재미없다	to be uninteresting
재미있다	to be interesting, fun
재즈	jazz
저	that (over there)
저 *hum.*	I (=나 *plain*)
저기	over there
저녁	1. evening; 2. dinner
저어	uh (expression of hesitation)
저희 *hum.*	we/us/our (=우리 *plain*)
적다	to be few, scarce
적어도	at least
전	before
전공	major
전공하다	to major

전기공학	electrical engineering	질문	question
전부	altogether	집	home, house
전화	telephone	짜다	to be salty
전화 번호	telephone number	짧다	to be short
전화비	telephone bill	째	ordinal numbers
전화하다	to make a telephone call	쪽	side, direction
점심	lunch	쭉	straight
점원	clerk, salesperson	쯤	about, around
정류장	(bus) stop	찍다	to take (a photo)
정말	really	차	tea
정치학	political science	차	car
제 *hum.*	my (=내 *plain*)	차다	to be cold
제일	first, most	차비	fare (bus, taxi)
조금	a little (=좀)	착하다	to be good-natured,
조심하다	to be careful		kindhearted
조용하다	to be quiet	참	1. really, truly;
졸다	to doze off		2. by the way
졸업(하다)	graduation	찾다	to find, look for
좀	a little (contraction of	책	book
	조금)	책방	bookstore
좁다	to be narrow	책상	desk
종업원	employee	처음	the first time
좋다	to be good, nice	천천히	slow(ly)
좋아하다	to like	첫	first
죄송하다	to be sorry	청바지	blue jeans
주	week	청소	cleaning
주다	to give	청소하다	to clean
주말	weekend	초등학교	elementary school
주무시다 *hon.*	to sleep (=자다 *plain*)	초등학생	elementary school
주문하다	to order		student
주소	address	축구	soccer
주스	juice	축하하다	to congratulate
주인공	main character	출구	exit
죽다	to die	춤추다	to dance
준비	preparation	춥다	to be cold
준비하다	to prepare	취미	hobby
중국	China	층	floor, layer (counter)
중식	Chinese-style (food)	치다	1. to play (tennis);
중에서	between, among		2. to play (piano, guitar)
중학교	middle school	치마	skirt
중학생	middle school student	친구	friend
즐겁다	to be joyful	친절하다	to be kind, considerate
지금	now	칠판	blackboard
지난	last, past	카드	card
지내다	to get along	캐나다	Canada
지다	to lose	캠퍼스	campus
지도	map	커피	coffee
지하철	subway	커피숍	coffee shop, café
직접	directly	컴퓨터	computer

컴퓨터 랩	computer lab	피우다	to smoke
케이크	cake	피자	pizza
켜다	to play (violin)	하고	1. and (with nouns);
켤레	pair		2. with
코미디	comedy	하나	one
쿠바	Cuba	하다	to do
크게	loud(ly)	하루	(one) day
크다	to be big	하얗다	to be white
크리스마스	Christmas	하와이	Hawai'i
큰아버지	uncle (father's older	학교	school
	brother)	학기	semester, academic term
클래스	class	학년	school year
클래식	classical music	학비	tuition fees
클럽	club	학생	student
키	height	학생회관	student center
키가 작다	to be short	한	one (with counter)
키가 크다	to be tall	한국	Korea
타고 가다	to go riding	한국말	the Korean language
타고 다니다	to come/go riding	한국어	the Korean language
타고 오다	to come riding	한국학	Korean studies
타다	to get in/on, ride	한글	Korean alphabet
타이레놀	tylenol	한복	traditional Korean dress
태권도	Korean martial art	한식	Korean-style (food)
태어나다	to be born	한인타운	Koreatown
택시	taxi	한테	to (a person or an
택시비	taxi fare		animal)
테니스	tennis	한테서	from (a person or an
테니스장	tennis court		animal)
텔레비전	television	할머니	grandmother
토요일	Saturday	할아버지	grandfather
통화	phone call	햄버거	hamburger
트럭	truck	행복하다	to be happy
특히	particularly	헤드폰	headphones
틀다	to turn on, switch on,	형	the older brother of a
	play (music)		male
파랗다	to be blue	형님 *hon.*	the older brother of a
파티	party		male
팔다	to sell	형제	sibling(s)
펜	pen	호선	subway line
펴다	to open, unfold	호주	Australia
편리하다	to be convenient	홍콩	Hong Kong
편지	letter	화요일	Tuesday
편하다	to be comfortable,	화장실	bathroom, restroom
	convenient	후	after
풋볼	football	휴게실	lounge
프랑스	France	휴일	holiday, day off
피곤하다	to be tired	흐리다	to be cloudy
피아노	piano	힘(이) 들다	to be hard

English-Korean Glossary

0 (zero)	공; 영	attached to a	씨
1	일	person's name	
2	이	for courtesy	
3	삼	attend [to]	다니다
4	사	Australia	호주
about	쯤	autumn	가을
above	위	back [the]	뒤
academic term	학기	bad [to be]	나쁘다
accident	사고	bag	가방
action	액션	ballpoint pen	볼펜
address	주소	bank	은행
after	후	barbecued spareribs	갈비
after a long time	오래간만	baseball	야구
afternoon	오후	basketball	농구
again	다시	basketball game	농구 시합
age	나이; 연세 *hon.*	bath	목욕
airplane	비행기	bathe [to]	목욕하다
airport	공항	bathroom	화장실
a little	조금 (= 좀)	be [to]	이다 (equation)
a little	좀 (= 조금)	be [to]	없다 (existence)
a little later	이따가	be [to]	계시다 *hon.*
all	다; 모두		(existence)
all right [to be]	괜찮다	be [to]	있다 (existence)
already	벌써	be [to not]	아니다 (negative
altogether	전부		equation)
also	또	be [to not]	~지 않다
also (particle)	도	be so [to]	그렇다
a.m.	오전	beach	바닷가
among	중에서	because of	때문에
and	그리고	become [to]	되다
and	또	before	전
and	와/과 (with nouns)	begin [to]	시작하다
and	하고 (with nouns)	behind	뒤
animal	마리 (counter)	below	밑, 아래
answer	답; 대답	beside	옆
apartment	아파트	between	사이
architecture	건축학	between	중에서
around	쯤	beverage	음료수
arrive [to]	도착하다	*bibimbap*	비빔밥
Asian studies	동양학	bicycle	자전거
ask [to]	묻다	big [to be]	크다
ask a favor [to]	부탁하다	biology	생물학
at	에서 (dynamic	birthday	생일; 생신 *hon.*
	location)	bitter [to be]	쓰다
at	에 (static location)	black [to be]	까맣다
at	에 (time)	blackboard	칠판
at least	적어도	black color	까만색 (=까망)

bland [to be]	싱겁다	change [to]	갈아 타다
blocked [to be]	막히다		(vehicles)
blue [to be]	파랗다	change [to]	바꾸다
blue jeans	청바지	chapter	과
body	몸	chat	이야기(=얘기)
book	책	chat [to]	얘기하다,
bookstore	책방, 서점		이야기하다
bored [to be]	심심하다	cheap [to be]	싸다
born [to be]	태어나다	check	계산서
borrow [to]	빌리다	check out [to]	알아보다
Boston	보스톤	Chicago	시카고
bottom [the]	밑, 아래	child	아이
bowling	볼링	China	중국
box	박스	Chinese-style	중식 (food)
breakdown	고장	choose [to]	고르다
breakfast	아침	Christmas	크리스마스
bring [to]	갖고 오다	church	교회
bring and put	갖다 놓다	cigarette	담배
down [to]		city	도시
Broadway Theater	브로드웨이 극장	city hall	시청
brush one's	이(를) 닦다	city hall station	시청역
teeth [to]		class	반; 수업; 클래스
building	건물, 빌딩	classical music	클래식
bulgogi	불고기	classroom	교실
bus	버스	clean [to]	청소하다
bus stop	정류장	clean [to be]	깨끗하다
busy [to be]	바쁘다	cleaning	청소
but	그런데; 그렇지만	clerk	점원
buy [to]	사다	clock	시계
buy one's groceries	장(을) 보다	close [to]	덮다
by means of	(으)로	close [to be]	가깝다
by the way	그런데; 참	clothes	옷
café	커피숍	clothing store	옷가게
cake	케이크	cloudy [to be]	흐리다
campus	캠퍼스	club	클럽
Canada	캐나다	coffee	커피
cannot	못	coffee shop	커피숍
cap	모자	cold [to be]	차다; 춥다
capital (city)	수도	cold noodle dish	냉면
car	차	collect [to]	모으다
card	카드	college	대학, 대학교
careful [to be]	조심하다	college student	대학생
care of health	몸조리	color	색 (=색깔)
carry around	갖고 다니다	come [to]	오다
catch [to]	잡다	come back [to]	돌아오다
catch a cold [to]	감기에 걸리다	come in [to]	들어오다
cent	센트	come on foot	걸어오다
center [the]	가운데	come out [to]	나오다
chair	의자	come out to greet	마중 나오다
change [to]	갈아 입다 (clothes)	someone [to]	

come riding [to]	타고 오다	die [to]	죽다
comedy	코미디	different [to be]	다르다
comfortable	편하다	difficult [to be]	어렵다
comic book	만화책	diligently	열심히
computer	컴퓨터	dinner	저녁
computer lab	컴퓨터 랩	direction	쪽
concert	음악회	directly	직접
congested [to be]	막히다	dirty [to be]	더럽다
congratulate [to]	축하하다	dishwashing	설거지
considerate [to be]	친절하다	dislike [to]	싫어하다
contact	연락	distance	거리
contact [to]	연락하다	do [to]	하다
convenient [to be]	편리하다; 편하다	do [to not]	~지 않다
cook [to]	요리하다	doctor	의사
cooked rice	밥	dog	개
cooking	요리	dollar	불 (=달러)
cool [to]	시원하다	do not	안
cost money [to]	돈이 들다	door	문
cost of living	물가	dormitory	기숙사
country	나라	doze off [to]	졸다
course	과목; 수업	drama	드라마
cover [to]	덮다	draw [to]	그리다
cracker	과자	dream a dream	꿈(을) 꾸다
cross [to]	건너다	drink [to]	마시다
crowded [to be]	복잡하다	drive [to]	운전하다
Cuba	쿠바	driver	기사
culture	문화	drugstore	약국
cup	잔	drum	드럼
customer	손님	during	동안
cut [to]	자르다	each other	서로
cut something	잘라 드리다 *hon.*	early	일찍
(for someone) [to]		earn [to]	벌다
cut something	잘라 주다	earn money [to]	돈을 벌다
(for someone) [to]		earring	귀걸이
dance [to]	춤추다	East Coast	동부
date [to]	데이트(하다)	East Gate Market	동대문 시장
daughter	딸; 따님 *hon.*	East Hall	이스트 홀
dawn	새벽	easy [to be]	쉽다
day	날	eat [to]	먹다; 드시다 *hon.*
day	일 (counter)	eat out [to]	외식하다
day after tomorrow	모레	economics	경제학
day off	휴일	education	교육학
dear (spouse)	여보	electrical	전기공학
Dear me!	어머	engineering	
delicious [to be]	맛있다	elementary school	초등학교
delicious [to be not]	맛없다	elementary school	초등학생
department store	백화점	student	
desk	책상	elevator	엘리베이터
dictionary	사전	email	이메일

employee	종업원	freshman	1학년
engagement	약속	Friday	금요일
English language	영어	friend	친구
enter [to]	들어가다	from	한테서 (a person
entrance	입구		or an animal)
et cetera	등	from	에서 (location)
evening	저녁	from	부터 (time)
event	일	from next time	다음부터(는)
every day	날마다; 매일	front	앞
every month	매달	fruit	과일
every week	매주	fun [to be]	재미있다
every year	매년	galbi	갈비
exam	시험	game	게임; 경기(match)
excited [to be]	신나다	get [to]	되다
excused [to be]	실례하다	get along [to]	지내다
exercise	운동	get in [to]	타다
exercise [to]	운동하다	get off [to]	내리다
exit	출구	get on [to]	타다
expensive [to be]	비싸다	get up [to]	일어나다
eyeglasses	안경	gift	선물
eyes	눈	gimbap	김밥
face	얼굴	girlfriend	여자 친구
fall	가을	give [to]	주다; 드리다 hum.
family	가족	give a present [to]	선물하다
far [to be]	멀다	glad [to be]	반갑다
fare	차비 (bus, taxi)	glass	잔
fast	빨리	gloves	장갑
fast [to be]	빠르다	go [to]	가다
father	아버지	go down [to]	내려가다
feast	잔치	go on foot [to]	걸어가다
feeling	기분	go out [to]	나가다
few [to be]	적다	go out to greet	마중 나가다
find [to]	찾다	someone [to]	
find out [to]	알아보다	go riding [to]	타고 가다
finished [to be]	끝나다	go up [to]	올라가다
first	제일; 첫	gold ring	금반지
first birthday	돌	golf	골프
first time	처음	good [to be]	좋다
floor	층 (counter)	good-natured [to be]	착하다
flower	꽃	grab [to]	잡다
flower shop	꽃집	graduate [to]	졸업하다
following	다음	graduate school	대학원
food	음식	graduate student	대학원생
foot	발	graduation	졸업
football	풋볼	grandfather	할아버지
for	에	grandmother	할머니
for a short time	잠깐만	green tea	녹차
France	프랑스	greet [to]	인사하다
frequently	자주	greeting	인사

grow up [to]	자라다	I	나; 저 *hum.*
guest	손님	ice hockey	아이스하키
guitar	기타	in	에서 (dynamic location)
hair	머리		
half	반	in	에 (static location)
hamburger	햄버거	in	에 (time)
happy [to be]	행복하다	Incheon	인천
hard [to be]	힘(이) 들다	including	까지
hat	모자	inconvenient [to be]	불편하다
have [to]	있다	inquire [to]	물어보다
have [to not]	없다	inside	안
have a cold [to]	감기에 걸리다	instant noodles	라면 (ramen)
have a full stomach [to]	배(가) 부르다	interesting [to be]	재미있다
		internet	인터넷
have a meal [to]	식사하다	intersection	사거리
Hawai'i	하와이	interview	인터뷰
head	머리	I see	네, 예
headphones	헤드폰	item	개 (counter)
healthy [to be]	건강하다	It's hard to say	글쎄요
height	키	Italy	이태리
hello	여보세요 (on the phone)	Japan	일본
		Japanese-style	일식 (food)
help [to]	돕다	jazz	재즈
here	여기	joyful [to be]	즐겁다
high school	고등학교	juice	주스
high school student	고등학생	junior	3학년
hike [to]	등산하다	just	그냥
hiking	등산	karaoke	노래방
history	역사	kid	아이
hobby	취미	*kimchi*	김치
holiday	휴일	kind [to be]	친절하다
home	집; 댁 *hon.*	kindhearted [to be]	착하다
hometown	고향	kitchen	부엌
homework	숙제	know [to]	알다
homework [to do]	숙제하다	know [to not]	모르다
honey	여보	Korea	한국
Hong Kong	홍콩	Koreatown	한인타운
horror movie	공포 영화	Korean alphabet	한글
hot [to be]	덥다; 뜨겁다	Korean language	한국말; 한국어
hot shredded beef soup	육개장	Korean martial art	태권도
		Korean-style	한식 (food)
hour	시	lab	랩
house	집; 댁 *hon.*	last	지난
how	어떻게	last night	어젯밤
how [to be]	어떻다	last year	작년
however	그런데; 그렇지만	late	늦게
how long/much	얼마; 얼마나	late [to be]	늦다
how many	몇	later	나중에, 이따가
hungry [to be]	배(가) 고프다	law	법학

layer	층 (counter)	meal	식사; 밥
learn [to]	배우다	mean [to]	뜻하다
leave [to]	남기다 (a message)	meantime	그동안
left side	왼쪽	mechanical	기계 공학
lend [to]	빌려주다	engineering	
less	덜	meet [to]	만나다
lesson	과	menu	메뉴
letter	편지	merchandise	물건
library	도서관	message	메시지
life	생활	Mexico	멕시코
like [to]	좋아하다	middle [the]	가운데
linguistics	언어학	middle school	중학교
listen [to]	듣다	middle school	중학생
literature	문학	student	
live [to]	살다	million	백만
living	생활	minute	분 (counter)
long [to be]	길다	mister	아저씨
long time	오래	mom	엄마
look [to]	보다	Monday	월요일
look around [to]	구경하다	money	돈
look for [to]	찾다	month	달 (counter)
Los Angeles	로스앤젤레스	month	월 (counter)
lose [to]	지다	more	더
love [to]	사랑하다	morning	아침
loud [to be]	크다	most	제일
loud(ly)	크게	most [the]	가장
lounge	휴게실 (=라운지)	mother	어머니
lunch	점심	move [to]	이사하다
magazine	잡지	movie	영화
mail [to]	부치다 (a letter,	movie theater	극장
	parcel)	much	많이
main character	주인공	much [to be]	많다
major	전공	music	음악
major [to]	전공하다	musical instrument	악기
make [to]	만들다	musical	연주
make a telephone	전화하다	performance	
call [to]		my	내; 제 *hum.*
make friends [to]	사귀다	*naengmyeon*	냉면
man	남자	name	이름; 성함 *hon.*
man of one's	아저씨	narrow [to be]	좁다
parents' age		near [to be]	가깝다
many [to be]	많이; 여러	nearby	근처
many [to be]	많다	necklace	목걸이
map	지도	neighborhood	동네
market	마켓	new	새
marketplace	시장	newly	새로
marriage	결혼	news	뉴스
married [to get]	결혼하다	newspaper	신문
match	경기	New Year	새해

New York	뉴욕	over there	저기
next	다음	painting	그림
next year	내년	pair	켤레
nice [to be]	좋다	pants	바지
night	밤	parents	부모님
no	아니요	park	공원
noisy [to be]	시끄럽다	particularly	특히
nothing but	밖에	party	잔치; 파티
novel	소설	pass away [to]	돌아가시다 *hon.*
now	지금; 이제	past	지난
number	번호	pay [to]	돈을 내다
number	번 (counter)	peace [in]	안녕히
number of times	번 (e.g., 한 번)	pen	펜
object particle	을, 를	pencil	연필
occasionally	자주	people	사람
o'clock	시	people	명; 분 *hon.*(counter)
of	의	per	에
often	자주	perhaps	아마
oh! Oh my!	아; 어; 어머	person	사람
Dear me!		personality	성격
okay/OK	네 (=예)	phone call	통화
okay [to be]	괜찮다	photo	사진
older brother of	오빠	physics	물리학
a female [the]		piano	피아노
older brother of	형	picture	그림; 사진
a male [the]		pizza	피자
older brother of	형님 *hon.*	place	곳; 군데; 데
a male [the]		plan	계획
older sister of	언니	plan [to]	계획하다
a female [the]		play	연극
older sister of	누나	play [to]	틀다 (music);
a male [the]			치다 (tennis);
Olympic	올림픽		놀다; 켜다 (violin);
on	에 (static location)		하다 (game,
on	에 (time)		sports)
one	하나	playground	운동장
one	한 (with counter)	plural particle	들
one day	하루	political science	정치학
one portion	일 인 분	population	인구
only	만; 밖에	post office	우체국
open [to]	열다; 펴다	practice	연습
oral exam	구두 시험	practice [to]	연습하다
order [to]	시키다, 주문하다	preparation	준비
ordinal numbers	째/번째	prepare [to]	준비하다
other side [the]	건너편	present	선물
our	우리; 저희 *hum.*	president	대통령
outside	밖	presidential election	대통령 선거
over [to be]	끝나다	pretty [to be]	예쁘다
oversleep	늦잠	price	값

probably	아마
professor	교수님
professor's office	연구실
promise	약속
psychology	심리학
put forth effort	수고하다
put on [to]	입다 (clothes)
put something down for someone [to]	놓아 주다
question	질문
quick(ly)	어서
quickly	빨리
quiet [to be]	조용하다
radio	라디오
rain	비
rain [to]	비(가) 오다
read [to]	읽다
reading	독서
really	아주; 정말; 참
really [(not)]	별로
receive [to]	받다
red [to be]	빨갛다
red-pepper paste	고추장
refreshing [be]	시원하다
relationship	사이
repeat after [to]	따라하다
resemble [to]	닮다
rest [to]	쉬다
restaurant	식당, 음식점
restroom	화장실
return [to]	돌아오다
return something [to]	돌려 주다; 돌려 드리다 hon.
review	복습
review [to]	복습하다
rice	밥
ride [to]	타다
ride regularly [to]	타고 다니다
right side	오른쪽
ring	반지
road	길
rock music	록
rock-paper-scissors	가위바위보
room	방
roommate	룸메이트
run [to]	뛰다
Russia	러시아
sad [to be]	슬프다

sale	세일
salesperson	점원
salty [to be]	짜다
sandwich	샌드위치
Saturday	토요일
scarce [to be]	적다
school	학교
school vacation	방학
school year	학년
season	계절
seat	자리
second [the]	두 번째
see [to]	보다; 뵙다 hum.
seen [to be]	보이다
select [to]	고르다
sell [to]	팔다
semester	학기
send [to]	보내다
senior	4학년
Seol-ak Mount	설악산
Seoul	서울
service	서비스
several	여러
shirt	셔츠
shoes	신발
shop [to]	쇼핑하다
shopping	쇼핑
short [to be]	짧다; (키가) 작다
shower	샤워
sibling(s)	형제
sick [to be]	아프다
side	쪽
side [the]	옆
side dishes	반찬
sightsee [to]	구경하다
signify [to]	뜻하다
sing [to]	노래 부르다
singer	가수
sit [to]	앉다
size	사이즈
ski [to]	스키 타다
skirt	치마
sleep	잠
sleep [to]	자다; 주무시다 hon.
slow(ly)	천천히
small [to be]	작다 (in size)
smoke [to]	피우다
sneakers	운동화
snow	눈

snow [to]	눈(이) 오다	supermarket	슈퍼
so	그래서	sweater	스웨터
soccer	축구	sweet [to be]	달다
socks	양말	swim [to]	수영하다
soft tofu stew	순두부 찌개	swimming	수영
sometimes	가끔	swimming pool	수영장
son	아들	switch [to]	바꾸다
song	노래	switch on [to]	틀다 (music)
soon	금방	Sydney	시드니
sophomore	2학년	table	상; 테이블
sorry [to be]	미안하다; 죄송하다	take [to]	찍다 (a photo)
sour [to be]	시다	take [to]	걸리다 (time)
soybean-paste stew	된장찌개	take [to]	갖고 가다
spacious [to be]	넓다	take a course	듣다
spaghetti	스파게티	take a shower	샤워하다
Spain	스페인	take off [to]	벗다
speak [to]	말하다	take something to	갖다 주다
speech	말; 말씀 hon.	someone [to]	갖다 드리다 hum.
spend time [to]	보내다	take trouble [to]	수고하다
spicy [to be]	맵다	talk	이야기 (=얘기)
sports	스포츠	talk [to]	이야기하다
sports shoes	운동화		(=얘기하다)
spot	군데	tall [to be]	키가 크다
spring	봄	tasteless	맛없다
stairs	계단	taxi	택시
stamp	우표	taxi fare	택시비
station	역	tea	차
stay [to]	계시다 hon.	teach [to]	가르치다
still	아직	teacher	선생님
stockings	양말	teacher's wife	사모님
stomach	배	telephone	전화
store	가게	telephone bill	전화비
straight	똑바로; 쭉	telephone number	전화 번호
street	거리; 길	television	텔레비전
stress	스트레스	tennis	테니스
student	학생	tennis court	테니스장
student center	학생회관	test	시험
study	공부	textbook	교과서
study [to]	공부하다	than	보다
subject	과목	thankful [to be]	감사하다; 고맙다
subject particle	이/가; 께서 hon.	that	그
subway	지하철	that (over there)	저
subway line	호선	then [(if so)]	그럼
suffix inserted	이	there	거기
after a Korean first		therefore	그래서
name that ends in		these days	요즘
a consonant		thing	거 (= 것)
summer	여름	thirsty [to be]	목(이) 마르다
Sunday	일요일	this	이

this	이거 (=이것)
this time	이번
this way	이쪽으로
this year	올해
thread	실
thriller	스릴러
through	까지 (time)
Thursday	목요일
time	때; 시간
tired [to be]	피곤하다
to	으로
to (a person or an animal)	한테
to (a person)	께 hon.
to (destination)	에
to (time)	까지
today	오늘
together	같이
Tokyo	도쿄
tomorrow	내일
too	또
too (particle)	도
too much	너무
tooth	이
topic particle	은/는 ('as for')
top side [the]	위
toward	으로
traditional Korean dress	한복
traffic	교통
traffic light	신호등
train	기차
travel	여행
travel [to]	여행하다
truck	트럭
truly	참
Tuesday	화요일
tuition fees	학비
turn [to]	돌다
turn into [to]	되다
turn on [to]	틀다 (music)
two	둘
two	두 (with counter)
Tylenol	타이레놀
uh	저어
umbrella	우산
uncle	큰아버지 (father's older brother)
uncomfortable [to be]	불편하다

undesirable [to be]	싫다
unfold [to]	펴다
uninteresting [to be]	재미없다
Union Building	유니온 빌딩
United Kingdom	영국
United States	미국
university	대학; 대학교
until	까지 (time)
upright	똑바로
up to	까지 (location)
us	우리; 저희 hum.
use [to]	쓰다
usually	보통
Vancouver	밴쿠버
very	아주
very much	굉장히; 무척
vicinity	근처
violin	바이올린
visible [to be]	보이다
voice	목소리
volume	권 (counter)
wait [to]	기다리다
walk [to]	걷다
walk regularly [to]	걸어다니다
want to [to]	싶다
warm [to be]	따뜻하다
wash [to]	빨래하다 (laundry)
wash [to]	설거지하다 (dishes)
wash [to]	세수하다 (face)
wash [to]	손(을) 씻다 (hands)
watch	시계
watch [to]	보다
water	물
we	우리; 저희 hum.
wealthy person	부자
wear [to]	끼다 (glasses, gloves, rings)
wear [to]	신다 (footwear)
wear [to]	쓰다 (headgear)
wear [to]	입다 (clothes)
weather	날씨
Wednesday	수요일
week	주
weekend	주말
well	잘
Well; It's hard to say	글쎄요
well [to be]	안녕하다
Western-style	양식 (food)
what	몇

what	무슨	woman	여자
what	무엇 (=뭐)	won	원 (Korean currency)
what kind of	무슨; 어떤	words	말; 말씀 *hon.*
what place	어디	work	일
what's the matter	웬일	work [to]	일하다
when	언제	work [to not]	놀다
where	어디	World Cup	월드컵
which	어느	write [to]	쓰다
which	어떤	year	년 (counter)
white [to be]	하얗다	years old	살 (counter)
who	누구	yellow [to be]	노랗다
who	누가 (누구+가)	yes	네 (=예)
why	왜	yesterday	어제
wide [to be]	넓다	yet	아직
win [to]	이기다	you	너
winter	겨울	young [to be]	어리다
with	하고	younger brother	남동생
without any special reason	그냥	younger sibling	동생
		younger sister	여동생
without doing anything further	그만	youngest child	막내